The Hulton Getty Picture Collection

The German Millennium

1,000 Remarkable Years
of Incident and Achievement

The Hulton Getty Picture Collection

The German
Millennium

1,000 Remarkable Years
of Incident and Achievement

Nick Yapp

KÖNEMANN

Frontispiece: Marlene Dietrich went to America in 1930,
but it is hard to disassociate her smoke-stained voice from the clubs of pre-war Berlin,
the city in which she was born. Aloof, world-weary, sophisticated, androgynous,
the adjectives piled up to describe one of the true stars in the Hollywood firmament.

First published in 2000 by Könemann Verlagsgesellschaft mbH,
Bonner Strasse 126, D-50968 Köln

This book was produced by The Hulton Getty Picture Collection,
Unique House, 21–31 Woodfield Road, London W9 2BA

Design: Mick Hodson and Alan Price
Project manager and editor: Richard Collins
Picture editor: Franziska Payer Crockett
Copy editor: Christine Collins
Proof reader and indexer: Liz Ihre
Editorial assistance: Tom Worsley, Gill Hodson
Scanning: Antonia Hille, Dave Roling, Mark Thompson

Publishing director: Peter Feierabend

Typesetting by Mick Hodson Associates
Colour separation by Omniascanners srl
Printed and bound by Star Standard Industries Ltd
Printed in Singapore
ISBN 3-8290-6013-0
10 9 8 7 6 5 4 3 2 1

CONTENTS

GENERAL INTRODUCTION

It has been Germany's good luck and misfortune, at one and the same time, to be situated at the heart of historically the most volatile continent in the world. Warriors and thinkers have clashed on German soil with exhausting regularity and equal ferocity over the past one thousand years, and often in disputes that were home-grown.

In the past five hundred years, German intellects have created Protestantism, *The Critique of Pure Reason*, psychoanalysis, surrealism and socialism. The first of these tore apart the old medieval world of Roman Catholicism. The last hurled a challenge to modern capitalism that has not yet been fully resolved – to the relief of some, and the exasperation of many.

Conflict, whether of mind or body, has been at the heart of German existence. It has destroyed the peace and, indeed, the lives of many German people, but has also fuelled many of their greatest achievements. Over the centuries, Germany has produced the first and finest automobiles, the first modern printing press, the diesel engine, rocket propulsion, meat extract, the first X-ray machine, the symphony, the submarine, plus and minus signs, the revolver, Doc Martens and stained glass.

The landscape of Germany is built on a huge, almost continental scale – a land of mountain and forest, of the biggest river in Europe, of plains and marshes that stretch away over the horizon. It has been a land of distant frontiers, of border disputes, of invasions and wars. Establishing control over such a vast and disparate nation has always been a problem.

Dynasties have clashed, nations have fought bitter wars, brothers have taken arms against brothers – all to determine where German authority begins and ends. Within the space of a single lifetime, an inhabitant of Alsace could have changed nationality five times between 1870 and 1945.

German legends have been fed into art and literature – legends of the struggle of heroes to free the people from control by wizards and sorcerers, despots and tyrants. In much of German poetry, cinema and theatre there is the brooding presence of evil. And yet the sun bursts through – in comedy, lunacy, parody, and in a national delight in debunking the pompous and the authoritarian. On top of all this, it seems almost unfair that a single people should have been allowed to produce the Bach family, Haydn, Mozart, Beethoven, Weber, Schubert, the Schumanns, Wagner, Brahms, the Strausses, Mahler, Schönberg...and several dozen more.

It has taken the bravest of struggles, and heartache and suffering on an unmatched scale, to bring Germany to union and independence. Twice within the 20th century alone, Germany recovered from desolation. Perhaps no other nation in history has proved as clearly that it has the right, and the determination, to survive.

Map 1 The German Empire 1024–1125

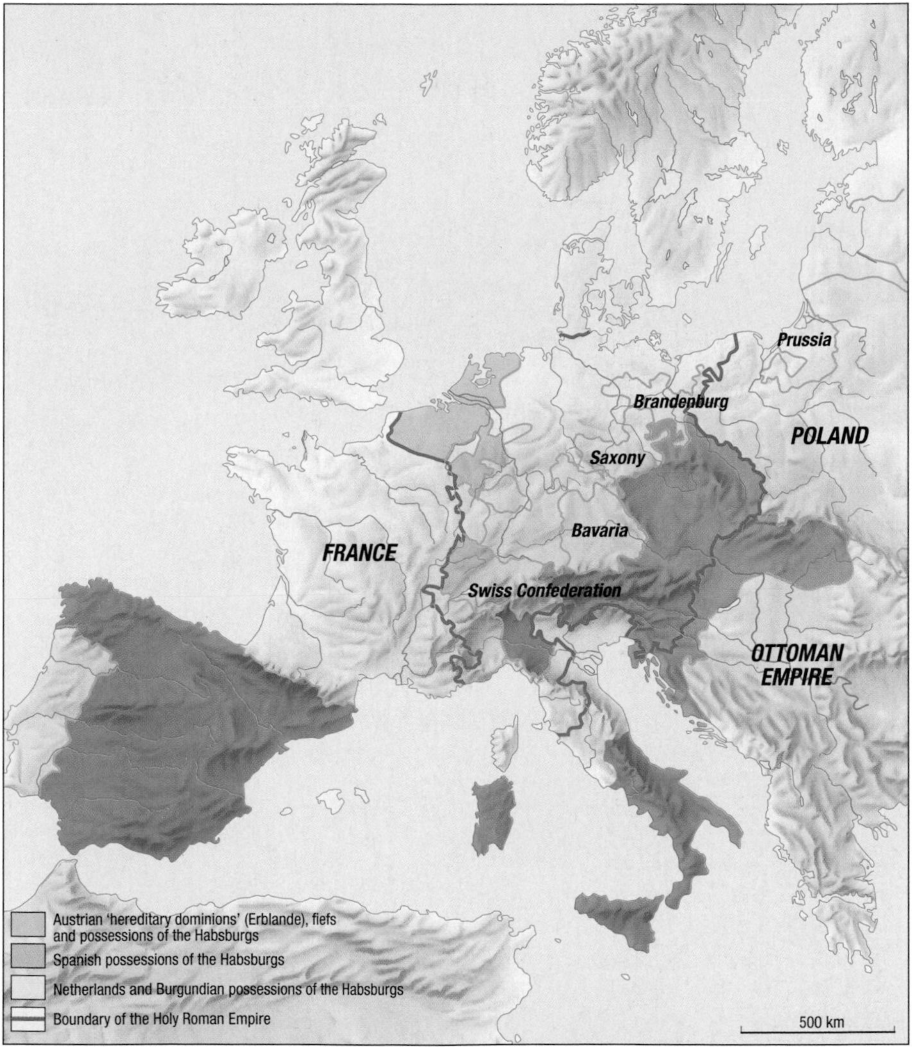

Map 2 The Reformation (Catholic/Protestant Divide)

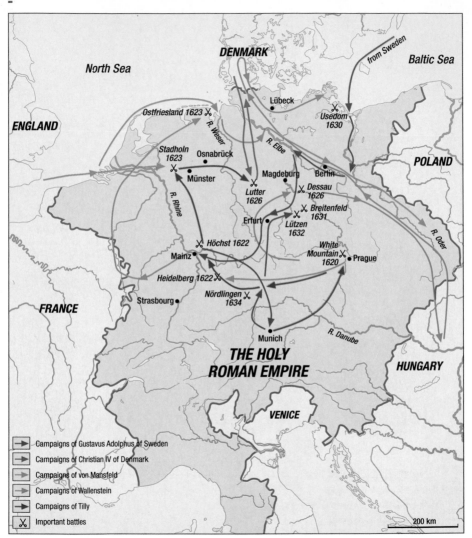

Map 3 The Extent of the German Empire under Karl V

Map 4 Germany after the Peace of Westphalia, 1648

Map 5 German Confederation in 1815

Map 6 Prussian–German Customs Union

DENMARK

SWEDEN

North Sea

Baltic Sea

Schleswig

Holstein · Lübeck

Hamburg **MECKLENBURG-SCHWERIN** Pomerania **West Prussia** **East Prussia**

OLDEN-BURG · Bremen

NETHER-LANDS

HANOVER R. Elbe **S** Berlin **I** **A**

P **R** **U** **Brandenburg** Posen

BRUNSWICK

RUSSIA

Westphalia **ANHALT**

BELGIUM Cologne · Langensalze 29.6.1866 Dresden Turnau 26.6.1866 **Silesia** R. Oder

R. Rhine Dermbach 4.7.1866 **THURINGIAN STATES** **SAXONY** Trautenau 27.6.1866

LUXEM-BURG Nassau **HESSE** Gitschin 29.6.1866 27.6.1866

Frankfurt · Hammelburg 10.7.1866 Prague · Königgrätz 3.7.1866

ALSACE-LORRAINE Tauberbischofsheim 24.7.1866

FRANCE **WÜRTTEM-BERG** **BAVARIA** R. Danube Vienna · **A** **U** **S** **T** **R** **I** **A**

BADEN Munich ·

Budapest ·

SWITZERLAND

Prussia

Austria-Hungary

North German Confederation and German Empire

- - - Area incorporated in North German Confederation in 1871 to form German Empire

✗ Important battles of the Prussian-Austrian War 1866

OTTOMAN EMPIRE

200 km

Map 7 Unification of Germany, 1866–1871

The Versailles settlements

	Lost by Germany 1919
	Demilitarised territory, March 1936 remilitarised
	Special regimes
	Frontiers of 1919

Territorial annexations by Nazi Germany 1935–1939

	March 1935	Saar territory by plebiscite		March 1939	Memel territory occupied
	March 1938	Austria seized		March 1939	Slovakia under German Protectorate
	October 1938	Sudetenland after Munich Agreement		September 1939	Danzig Free City and territory occupied
	March 1939	Bohemia and Moravia under German Protectorate		September 1939	Frontiers

Map 8 Germany, 1919–1939

Map 9 Germany Divided after 1945

North Sea

DENMARK

Baltic Sea

Schleswig-
Holstein   Lübeck

Hamburg

NETHER-
LANDS

Bremen

Mecklenburg-
Vorpommern

Lower Saxony

R. Elbe

FEDERAL

Brandenburg

R. Oder

POLAND

R. Rhine

North Rhine-
Westphalia

REPUBLIC

Saxony-
Anhalt

Berlin

Bonn

OF GERMANY

BELGIUM

Hessen

Thuringia

Saxony

LUX.

Rhine-
land
Palatinate

Frankfurt

Prague

Saar-
land

CZECH
REPUBLIC

FRANCE

Bavaria

Baden-
Württemberg

R. Danube

Munich

Vienna

SWITZERLAND

AUSTRIA

- - - Former division between East and West Germany

ITALY

100 km

Map 10 Germany in 2000

Introduction to
Period 1 – 1000–1519

At the beginning of the 19th century, the German poet, dramatist, scientist and court official Johann Wolfgang von Goethe wrote: 'Germany? But where is it? I know not how to find the country…'

Identifying their country had been a problem for generations of Germans. There had long been a German language, a German culture, German traditions, but no homeland. Part of the problem had been the absence of clearly defined 'natural' frontiers, the borders that other countries had regarded as those God intended. Britain was an island, clearly delineated. France looked to the sea, the Rhine and the Pyrenees as its rightful frontiers; Italy to the Alps and the sea; Spain to the Pyrenees and the sea. But Germany, until Goethe's own century, had always been a disparate collection of princedoms, archbishoprics, city states, and provinces – all loosely held together in alliances and federations that seldom had any permanence. The very name 'Germany' was derived not from a tribe or a territory, but from a language, and until 1400 the term 'deutsche Lande' (German lands) was much more commonly used than 'Deutschland'.

In the year 1000, these German lands had a

population of between 5 and 6 million souls. Most people lived on the land, in villages, hamlets, or isolated farmsteads surrounded by small clearings in the vast forests of central Europe. Houses were mere huts ; the only buildings of any substance were castles, churches, monasteries, the occasional royal palace, and some of the earliest of Germany's magnificent cathedrals – work began on Strasbourg Cathedral in 1015, and Augsburg Cathedral contained some of the first stained glass seen in Europe.

Average life expectancy was little better than thirty years. Most of the hardy and the lucky who survived infancy died somewhere between the ages of fourteen or forty, though famine and pestilence regularly wiped out entire communities, young and old alike. With the exception of pilgrims, few travelled outside their immediate neighbourhood. On holy days there was a welcome break from work, otherwise there was little relief from the grinding round of ploughing, sowing and, hopefully, harvesting.

The link between Germany and the Holy Roman Empire had already been forged in 962, when Otto I was crowned emperor by Pope John XII. It remained until 1806, shackling the German monarchy to the Church until the Reformation divided Germany into two warring religious camps. Otto died in 973, shortly after he had presided at a magnificent ceremony at Quedlinburg, where he received envoys from Rome, Bohemia, Poland, Hungary, Denmark, Russia, Byzantium, and even Africa. His successor, Otto II, died of malaria at the age of twenty-eight. Both Otto III and Heinrich II died childless, and the death of Heinrich in 1024 was followed by the election of Konrad II.

Germany now entered the period known as the High Middle Ages, a time of growth and expansion. More land was cultivated, even in the Slav lands to the east of the River Elbe. New colonies were founded in Silesia. The four-wheeled cart, pulled by horses instead of oxen, speeded the traffic of goods and allowed larger loads to be carried. The rotation of crops, and better ploughing methods, produced bigger harvests. The land supported more people and larger villages developed. German miners were much in demand. Silver-bearing lead ore and copper ore were found near Goslar in the Harz Mountains and near Freiberg. Industry was largely financed by Jewish moneylenders, who provided early venture capital. The first evidence of a walled ghetto comes from Speyer in 1084.

The already existing tradition of oral poetry began to give way to a flowering of written literature, the best known writers being Walther von der Vogelweide, Hartmann von Aue and Wolfram von Eschenbach. The *Minnesänger* (groups of travelling troubadours) created secular lyric poetry that spoke deeply of the pangs of unrequited love – an indispensable facet of the German code of chivalry. For the talented, it was possible to pursue a career as a professional poet at court, in a role similar to that of the jester. The first German versions of the legend of *Tristan und Isolde* and the *Nibelunglied* appeared in the late 12th century. Later, the *Minnesänger* were replaced by the *Meistersänger*, of whom the most famous was the Nuremberg cobbler Hans Sachs.

From 1200 until the coming of the Black Death in 1348, the population steadily grew, reaching 14 million by the mid-14th century. The plague struck a hammer blow on the German people, with over a quarter of the cultivated land lost due to shortage of labour. On the other hand, peasants were able to sell their labour at a higher price and their living conditions improved appreciably in the west and the south of the country.

Here there was also a considerable increase in the size and number of towns. Most had walls and fortifications, churches, castles, a splendid town hall, guild halls, and solid burgher houses. They were seen as places of walled safety from marauding bands of brigands and the rapacious ambitions of the princes. Town government was usually in the hands of a few wealthy families.

The towns were divided into two classes: the *Landesstadte* (subordinate to the local ruler), and the *Reichstadte* (imperial free cities, subordinate only to the emperor. As time went by, many of these towns banded together to form leagues – the Rhenish League in 1254, the Hanseatic League in 1358, and the Swabian League in 1376. As their power grew, they posed an increasing threat to many of the German princes, who joined together to defeat the Leagues in the Great Town War of 1387–8.

Other power groups were formed. Early in the 13th century the Religious Knights of the Teutonic Order established their own state in the north east, where the Marienburg, residence of the Grand Master of the Order, was founded in 1280. Two and a half centuries later, Albrecht von

Hohenzollern, Grand Master, adopted the Protestant religion and became the first German Duke of the hereditary Duchy of Prussia, and it was Prussia that was later to supply an answer to Goethe's plaintive question.

1
THE KINGDOM
OF THE SALIANS
1000–1106

Relations between pope and emperor were strained for much of
the reign of Heinrich IV. The young emperor's request for a
divorce from his child bride was refused by Pope Alexander II.
Seven years later, Alexander's successor, Gregory VII, threatened
Heinrich with excommunication if he did not abandon his
connection with those who had already been excommunicated.
Heinrich responded with the Negative Reply of Worms, which
accused Gregory of all manner of sins, including associating with
a married woman. Gregory immediately excommunicated the
young emperor. (*Left*) While under the pope's interdict, Heinrich
IV is refused admission to a monastery.

Introduction

For most of the 11th century, German emperors were faced with three major problems: establishing a working relationship with the papacy, maintaining peace and order within imperial territories, and protecting their frontiers from outside attack.

It was a tough task. A succession of popes played a highly political game, seeking to further their own power at the expense of that of the emperor. The threat of civil war was always present. And it was not easy to protect a kingdom that included an uneasy alliance of Burgundy, Upper and Lower Lorraine, Saxony, Franconia, Swabia, Bavaria and the disparate collection of the eastern marches. It took considerable diplomatic skill to keep on good terms with such neighbours as France and Flanders in the west, and Bohemia, Hungary and Poland in the east.

It was the custom for each emperor to travel

the length and breadth of his lands as early as possible in his reign, to assert his power and authority. The magnificent equestrian imperial statues in Bamberg and Magdeburg symbolise how important it was for an emperor to spend as much time as possible in the saddle. Those emperors who sought to establish a permanent court tended to lose control of the empire. When Heinrich IV built his royal stronghold and a string of mighty fortresses in the Harz Mountains, he provoked a civil war with the Saxons that cost him dear.

The bulk of the ordinary people, however, gave their loyalty to their Salian rulers, believing the emperors to have supernatural powers. The very earth covering the grave of Heinrich IV was believed to have magic properties, and the emperor's presence in a town or village was said to be a guarantee of fine weather, a good harvest and freedom from the plague.

In peaceful times there were more civilised pursuits on offer. Hunting was the most popular pastime for the wealthy. It was regarded as much a science as a sport, and was the subject of a great many books. To be equipped with superb horses and well-trained tassel-gentle or falcon-gentle was to bear the hallmarks of nobility itself.

The power of the Church was to be seen in the glories of Romanesque architecture – in hundreds of parish churches, and in the magnificent cathedrals of Speyer, Strasbourg, Essen, Mainz and Bamberg. The riches of emperor and Church alike were to be seen in the beautifully decorated and illustrated Gospels. Such richly-bound and impeccably written masterpieces as the Gospels of Bamberg and Heinrich III's Golden Gospel-book of 1050 were among the most splendid creations of early medieval Europe.

Charlemagne (*left*) was a man of energy, foresight and learning. He was emperor from 768 to 814, during which time he revived the Holy Roman Empire in the west, and fought over fifty campaigns for the protection of Christendom. His empire stretched from the Ebro to the Elbe, though later claims that he captured Jerusalem (*opposite, below*) are unfounded. (*Opposite, above left*) The imperial crown designed for the coronation of Otto the Great on 7 August 936. (*Opposite, above right*) The chapel of Charlemagne at Aachen Cathedral.

The imperial capital was established by Charlemagne at Aachen. In 796 Charlemagne began building his Palatine Chapel here (*left* and *opposite, above*). The building was supervised by Odo of Metz, a Frankish master builder, and was finally consecrated by Pope Leo III in 805. The prototype for the chapel was the church of San Vitale in Ravenna, a city looted by Charlemagne to obtain the Corinthian pillars for the Palatine Chapel at Aachen.

Charlemagne wished the chapel to combine earth and heaven, this world and the next. The chapel was thus designed as an octagon, a mixture of square and circle – the former symbolising worldly power, and the latter spiritual power. (*Right*) The Emperor Otto I, known as the Great. He was crowned in the Palatine Chapel, and presented to the people by the Archbishop of Mainz with the words: 'Behold, I bring you here King Otto, chosen by God... If you are satisfied with this choice show it by raising your right hands to heaven!' The people did as the archbishop bade them.

Otto's brothers – Thankmar and Heinrich – were among those who did not welcome the new emperor, and a civil war ensued. Thankmar died in 938, however, and Heinrich made peace with Otto. But it was not the end of Otto's troubles. A group of rebellious nobles joined the Hungarians in Liudolf's Rebellion of 953. Otto raised an army (*above, left*) and marched to defend his empire. He defeated the Hungarians at the Battle of Lechfeld in 955 (*below, left*).

Like Charlemagne, Otto was determined to promote and defend Christianity, especially in the eastern half of his empire. New bishoprics were founded in Aarhus, Ripen and Schleswig, and Magdeburg was elevated to an archbishopric. (*Above, right*) The Cathedral of Magdeburg in northern Germany. The building was commissioned by Otto to celebrate the victory of Lechfeld. (*Below, right*) Hrotsvitha, one of the earliest known German women poets. She lived from 932 to 1002 and was a Benedictine nun at Gandersheim, near Göttingen. Among her writings were Latin poems and six terentian comedies.

Otto III was only three years old when he became emperor. He spent most of his life in Rome, in a vain attempt to make it the capital of the empire. In 1001, the opposition of the people of Rome forced him to leave the city, and he died the following year. Two pages from the Golden Gospel-book of Otto III in the Bamberg treasury: (*above*) representatives from the Slavs, Germany, Gaul and Rome bring their gifts to the young emperor; (*opposite*) Otto III (centre) is seated in majesty to receive the homage of his nations. Around him are archbishops and other dignitaries carrying his coat of arms.

TIMELINES

MONARCHY	POLITICAL EVENTS	SCIENCE TECHNOLOGY	MUSIC	LITERATURE AND PHILOSOPHY	ART	ARCHITECTS AND ARCHITECTURE
LUDOLFINGER Heinrich II, der Heilige **1002/1014-24**				Otto III's Gospel Book, Reichenau		St. Michael, Hildesheim
						Speyer Cathedral
SALIER Konrad II **1024/1027-39**	First crusade leaves Cologne for Jerusalem			Heinrich III's 'Golden Gospel Book'		
	Germans expand eastward			Ezzo's Lied		Benedictine abbey Maria Laach
	Concordat of Worms allows election of bishops		Courtly music of the Minnesinger	Annolied		
					Stained glass windows of Augsburg Cathedral	Maulbronn monastery
Heinrich III **1039/1046-56**				Hartmann von Aue	Capital carvings	Murbach Marmoutier
	Emperor Friedrich I accepts papal authority			Walther von der Vogelweide	Door of Freiburg Cathedral	Strasbourg Cathedral
		Friedrich II founds university of Naples		Wolfram von Eschenbach	Stained glass	
Heinrich IV **1056/1084-1106**	Hanseatic League	Tinplating used on		Albertus Magnus Rudolf von Ems		Castel Del Monte, Puglia Cologne

Naumburg
Cathedral

Peter Parler

Ulrich Ensinger

Ulm Cathedral

Manessische
Liederhandschrift

Stefan Lochner

Michael Wolgemut

Tilmann
Riemenschneider

Hans Burgkmair

Albrecht Dürer

Lukas Cranach d.Ä.

Matthias Grünewald

Lohengrin

Meister Eckhart

Heinrich Seuse

Oswald von
Wolkenstein

Johannes Reuchlin

Sebastian Brant

Thyl Ulenspiegel

Ulrich von Hutten

Choral music
developed by Martin
Luther

armour in Bohemia

Ebstorf worldmap

Berthold Schwarz
invents gunpowder

Johannes Gutenberg
introduces printing
press with movable
type

Nikolaus Kopernikus
concludes that earth
orbits sun

Paracelsus discovers
hydrogen

Swiss Confederation
established

Jan Hus burnt at stake
in Constance for
heresy

Hussite wars break
out in Bohemia

Martin Luther's 95

RHEINFELDENER
(Rudolf von Rhein-
felden, Gegenkönig)
1077–80

LÜTZELBURGER
(Herman von Salm,
Gegenkönig) **1081–88**

SALIER
(Konrad, Sohn
Heinrichs IV,
Gegenkönig **1087–98**

Heinrich V
1106/1111–25

SUPPLINBURGER
Lothar III (von Supplin-
burg) **1125/1133–37**

The nave of the former collegiate church of St Georg, Reichenau, Oberzell. The murals on either side of the nave were painted by itinerant Byzantine-trained artists to depict the miracles of Christ. The set is complete, and is one of the oldest and finest in Europe. It dates from c. 1000.

(*Left*) The Benedictine monastery church of St Michael in Hildesheim. Building began in 1010 and was completed in 1033. The guiding spirit in its construction was Bishop Bernward, a keen patron of the arts. Most of the monks who built the church came from Cologne. The church is regarded as one of the finest examples of Ottonian architecture. (*Above*) A contemporary drawing of monks building a monastery. In the 11th century monasteries were among the richest and most advanced institutions in Germany.

145

BENEDICTVS VIII. Roman̄ẽ Co:
mitib? Tusculanis   creat? an.1012 Se:
dit an.ii.mens   Obijt die 27.Feb:
ruarij an.1024.   Vac.Sed.

Otto III was succeeded by Heinrich II (*right*), the son of Heinrich of Bavaria.
Heinrich spent much of his reign on military campaigns, leaving affairs of state
to his wife Kunigunde. He also drove Gregory VI, the antipope, from Rome
and restored Benedict VIII (*above*) to the papal throne. (*Opposite*) One of
the bas-reliefs in Bamberg Cathedral, founded by Heinrich II. It depicts the ordeal
of Kunigunde. Accused of adultery, she proved her innocence by walking over
red-hot ploughshares.

In many cases, the glory of Romanesque architecture throughout the early Holy Roman Empire was in the detail. Statues, pillar capitals, friezes, pulpits and other fittings reveal an unsurpassed level of craftsmanship. (*Above*) The font of the church at Freudenstadt in Baden-Württemberg. A man and a lion support the basilisks and bearded masks round the bowl. (*Opposite*) A detail from the door of St Maria im Kapitol, Cologne, c. 1065.

(*Left*) The greatest monument to the Salian dynasty – the magnificent Cathedral of St Maria and St Stephan at Speyer in the Saar. Speyer was one of the most important towns in the empire during the 11th century. Work began on the cathedral around the year 1030 under Konrad II and was completed by Heinrich IV.

The cathedral fell into disuse during the 17th century and remained a ruin for a hundred years. It was saved from destruction by Napoleon Bonaparte and was fully restored in the 19th century (*above*). (*Below, right*) Pope John XIX (seated) shown in an engraving from the late 18th century. If Pope John was notorious for the sale of hierarchical appointments, nothing suggests that he was acting untowardly when he crowned Konrad II Holy Roman emperor in 1027.

In 1046 Heinrich III (*opposite, above left*) was faced with the problem of adjudicating between the rival claims of three popes – Benedict IX, Sylvester III and Gregory VI – each one of them supported by powerful clans. At the Synod of Sutri (*left*) Heinrich deposed Benedict and Sylvester, and then went on to depose Gregory at a second synod in Rome. The emperor then selected Bishop Suidger of Bamberg, who took the title Clement II (*opposite, above right*).

The new pope celebrated his coronation mass in St Peter's on Christmas Day 1046, but died shortly after. Heinrich then appointed another German pope, Leo IX, a charming and cultured man who favoured reform. (*Right*) A drawing in an 11th-century manuscript of a king and minister dispensing justice.

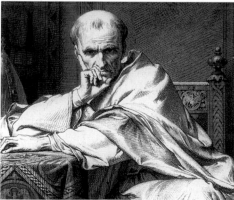

The struggle between pope and emperor came to a dramatic head in 1077. Gregory VII (*left*) had already excommunicated Heinrich IV, but the emperor and his wife and child journeyed barefoot to Canossa in Italy, where they waited for three days in the snow (*above*), seeking an audience with the pope. Forced against his will to display Christian compassion, Gregory consented to see Heinrich. The emperor prostrated himself in penance before the pope (*opposite*) and was received back into the Church. At the reconciliation feast that followed, however, Heinrich ate nothing.

Gregory was succeeded by Urban II (*left*), a strong-willed pope who managed to drive Heinrich IV and his armies from Italy. In 1095 Urban summoned the Council of Clermont (*opposite*), where he called for a Crusade to free Jerusalem from the 'infidel'. (*Above*) Peter the Hermit (kneeling) delivers a message from Simeon, Patriarch of Jerusalem, to Urban II.

For most inhabitants of the empire, the only alternative to a diet of bread, soup, porridge and an occasional piece of dried or salted meat was starvation. The rich, however, could indulge themselves in the occasional banquet (*above*). Even as early as the 11th century, this might include trenchers of beef, mutton, pork, poultry, venison, goat, pigeon, wild boar, rabbit and a variety of freshwater fish. The main problem, even for the rich, was how to take away the taste of the salt that had been used to preserve the food.

Hunting (*above, right*) was not only one of the favourite pastimes of the well-to-do, it also provided much-needed food for the heavy, uncovered tables at which they ate. Kings and nobles spent much of their leisure time in pursuit of boar and deer. For all that, hawking (*below, right*) was far more valued, for its skill and its ceremonial. A good falconer was among the most prized servants in a rich household.

Around the year 1000, German prospectors found silver-bearing lead ore and copper ore in the Harz Mountains. Within the next one hundred years, German miners had established a reputation as the finest in Europe. (*Opposite*) A German mine of the 11th century. (*Right*) A map showing some of the many mines in the valley of an unspecified river.

Nomi delle minere in Furtelbach.
Pozzo di S. Guglielmo. Rumpapumo.
S. Gio. Furstenbauu. Ferrea porta. Cō-
uito degli ylmefi, S. Martino, Tre paʒ
ʒi uniti, Forno, S. Sangue, Martello,
culto de compagni.
   Nella ualle Surbetʒ.
S. Michele, Verde Bofco, S. Giorgio
Copia, d' Argento.
   Nella ualle Prabegetʒ.
S. Filippo, S. Martino, Vite, Abiete uer
de, Armo monte, S. Vuillielmo.
   Nella ualle uecchia Eckirch.
Beata uergine al freddo Fonte, S. Gia-
cobo.

2
THE HOHENSTAUFENS
1106–1197

Pope Alexander III accepts the homage of the Emperor
Friedrich I (Friedrich Barbarossa), San Marco, 1177. The pair
were not well matched. Barbarossa originally refused to
recognise Alexander, and set up antipopes against him. Alexander
eventually defeated Barbarossa and forced him to sign the Treaty
of Venice, by which the emperor acknowledged Alexander as the
true pope, renounced his right to rule Rome, and made peace
with the Lombards and the Normans (the pope's allies).

Introduction

It was an age of building. There were new palaces for princes, bishops and emperors to flaunt their steadily increasing wealth, and new castles to protect their territories – of which perhaps the most beautiful was the Wartburg of the Landgrave of Thuringia. There were churches and cathedrals rising in splendour for the greater glory of God above the walls of Speyer, Mainz, Cologne and Worms. And there were monasteries and abbeys that were part fortress, part church and part farm.

Life slowly improved. There were new scientific techniques in agriculture – more efficient windmills, better methods of damming rivers to provide water and power for watermills, new ways of harnessing draught animals to pull carts, ploughs and harrows. The most advanced husbandry was often to be found in monasteries. By the end of the 12th century the Cistercians were successfully cross-breeding sheep to produce bigger, healthier animals.

The most memorable figure of the age was Hildegard of Bingen – mystic, poet, musician, apothecary, politician and diplomat. This remarkable woman acted as adviser to emperors, popes and archbishops, to St Bernard of Clairvaux and to Barbarossa himself. She was the author of scientific works (*Physica* and *Cause et cure*), a morality play (*Ordo virtutum*), an acclaimed book of poetry (*Symphonia armonie celestium revelationem* – *Symphony of the Harmonies of Celestial Revelations*), and many songs.

The Salian line came to an end with the death of Heinrich V in 1125. Heinrich spent the bulk of his seventeen-year reign at loggerheads with a succession of popes. In 1110, the pope proposed a division of the empire – Heinrich was to renounce all claim to participating in the appointment of bishops, and in return the Church would hand over its considerable imperial estates. It didn't work.

The Hohenstaufens faced much the same problems. When Heinrich died childless, there were three candidates to succeed him: Friedrich of Swabia (the Hohenstaufen candidate), Lothar of Saxony (a member of the ancient Welf family), and Leopold, Margrave of Austria. After bitter jockeying for power between Welf and Hohenstaufen, Friedrich's younger brother Konrad was elected.

His reign was disastrous. He plunged the empire into civil war, and led the ill-conceived and ill-organised Second Crusade of 1144. Few were sorry when Konrad died and was succeeded by Friedrich III of Swabia, better known as Barbarossa (Redbeard). Barbarossa spent most of his life fighting. He built a series of fortresses across Germany in an attempt to secure his hold over the empire, and then set off on the Crusade of 1188. He drowned while bathing in the River Saleph in Asia Minor, on his way to the Holy Land.

The old cathedral in Mainz burnt down in 1081. Heinrich IV immediately ordered that the new Cathedral of St Martin and St Stephan should be built in its place, a basilica with a nave, aisles and Romanesque vaults (*above*). Gothic additions were made later.

Heinrich V (*above, left*) was the last of the Salian dynasty. He married Matilda, daughter of Henry I of England (*above, right*). Both Heinrich IV and Heinrich V spent much of their reigns in a struggle for power against a succession of popes. In 1111 Heinrich V interrupted the investiture of Pope Paschal II and placed him under arrest (*right*).

The enmity between popes and emperors was temporarily solved by the wily diplomacy of Pope Calixtus II (*opposite, below right*). In 1121, Calixtus overthrew Heinrich V's candidate, Gregory VIII, and a year later forced Heinrich to sign the Concordat of Worms. By the terms of the Concordat, Heinrich agreed that in future emperors would present bishops only with their sceptres (symbols of their worldly rights and powers). The pope would give his bishops the ring and crozier (purely religious symbols).

After the proclamation of the Concordat, a mass was celebrated in the Cathedral of St Peter in Worms (*opposite*). Heinrich received the eucharist and the kiss of peace from the leader of the papal delegation, Cardinal Lambert of Ostia. A contemporary chronicler, Ekkehard of Aura, wrote that it was as though Christ's tunic had been repaired. (*Above*) A 12th-century drawing of a papal audience. The protocol of the papal court was strictly enforced, and its magnificence rivalled that of any emperor.

At the age of eight, Hildegard of Bingen (*above, left* and *right*) was sent by her parents to the Benedictine community of nuns at Disibodenberg. She stayed there for the next seventy-four years, becoming abbess in 1141. Her two major scientific works – *Liber Scrivias* and *Liber Simplicis Medicinale* – are the earliest surviving scientific books by a woman, though her Latin was not good, and she needed the help of scribes in their composition.

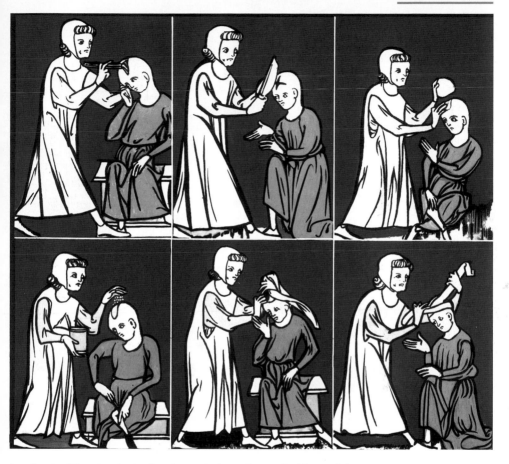

An early series of illustrations showing the major steps in the use of a trepan (saw) for a surgical operation. Surgeons learnt their craft as apprentices, few studied medicine at university. They were called upon to remove stones, lymph glands, fistulas and ulcers; to dress wounds with white of egg and finely ground flour; to set broken bones; and even to treat cancer and hernias. Of those patients who survived the surgeon's knife, some 50 per cent died of post-operative infection.

The Cistercian abbey of Maulbronn (*opposite*) was a completely enclosed and self-sufficient community in the 12th century. The abbey church possessed a fine porch at its west entrance, called a 'galilee' or 'paradise' (*right*). (*Below*) The Benedictine church of the monastery of Maria Laach, built in the late 12th century.

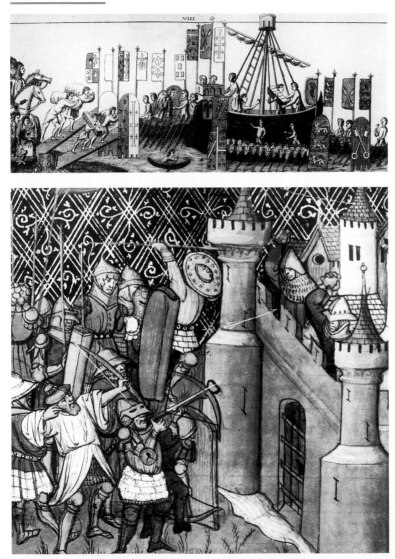

Men responded to the call to go on a Crusade for many reasons: to escape debts or an unhappy marriage, to receive the Church's blessing, for plunder, for excitement. (*Above, left*) The banners of the pope, the emperor, France, England, Anjou and Sicily are unfurled on board a ship embarking for the Holy Land, 1190. (*Below, left*) Crusaders assault a city in the Holy Land. Their lack of success in the late 12th century was attributed by one chronicler to a lack of truly religious men: 'In their places a wicked generation has grown, sinful sons, falsifiers of the Christian faith...'

In 1188, at an Assembly in Mainz, the Emperor Friedrich Barbarossa (*right*) proposed a new Crusade to the Holy Land. This was to be a well-planned military operation, rather than an eager expression of religious zeal. He assembled a large army at Regensburg and set off on the long march to Jerusalem. The following year, however, Friedrich was drowned while swimming in the River Saleph in Asia Minor. Like so many of its predecessors, the Crusade subsequently failed.

Many Crusaders, who had set out in such splendid armies (*opposite, above*), experienced a crisis of confidence when they failed to recover Jerusalem for Christendom. Some stayed, manning distant outposts, maintaining the presence of the Holy Cross in Asia Minor. The greatest of these outposts was the Krak des Chevaliers in Syria (*right and opposite, below*). It was built on the site of a native fortress and occupied by the Knight Hospitallers of Saint John from 1142 until its fall in 1271, and was described by an Arab writer as 'a bone in the throat of the Moslems...'

One of the finest examples of Hohenstaufen castles is the Ulrichsburg at Ribeauville (*right*). Perched on a barely accessible mountain top, it was crowned with an almost impenetrable keep. Successive emperors built such castles as strongholds to which they could retire when faced with rebellion or disorder, and also as secure bases from which they could attack over-mighty vassals or invaders.

Strategically weaker, but often far grander and more comfortable, were the imperial palaces. Little remains today of the imperial palace at Gelnhausen (*above*), but in its prime it had a large hall, covered promenades, extensive grounds, a farm, and its own chapel. Like the castles and fortresses, such palaces were generously sprinkled throughout the imperial domains.

potentissim̄ʳ Ĩpator   henyrg stoliū ε excerciū ffieri cubp

Marchili̅ʳ ſeneſcalc̄ʳ

boemij

bannarienſes

Friedrich Barbarossa was succeeded as emperor by his son, Heinrich VI (*below*). (*Left*) The Imperial Review of the Fleet. Heinrich is in the centre, with the Markward of Annweiler, Commander of the Fleet, to his right. On Heinrich's left are the imperial troops – mailed infantry, Bohemian archers with longbows, and Bavarian soldiers with crossbows.

In 1192, Heinrich was in desperate need of money to raise an army to fight Tancred, King of Sicily. He was saved by an unusual stroke of luck. While on his way back from an unsuccessful Crusade, Richard of England was taken prisoner by Leopold of Austria – a man whom he had insulted in the Holy Land. Leopold handed Richard over to Heinrich, who demanded, and received, a vast ransom from England for Richard's return. (*Above*) An illustration from the *Liber ad honorem Augusti* by Peter of Eboli. It shows Richard kissing the feet of Heinrich, while a servant holds the pilgrim's dress that Richard has just taken off.

(*Left*) Friedrich I (Barbarossa) sits on the imperial throne, with his son Heinrich on his left, and Herzog Friedrich of Swabia on his left. For all the attempts made to establish a hereditary dynasty by both Salians and Hohenstaufens, the unique system within the Holy Roman Empire made it impossible ever to be certain who would succeed on the death of an emperor. Heinrich VI was one of the few cases of a son succeeding his father.

(*Above*) A dramatic depiction of the struggle between Pope Alexander III and the Emperor Friedrich Barbarossa. In 1167 Barbarossa entered Rome in triumph, forcing Alexander to flee disguised as a humble pilgrim. An outbreak of malaria destroyed much of Barbarossa's army, and the Emperor in turn had to leave Italy. He returned in 1174, but his small force was defeated by the Milanese, and Barbarossa had no choice but to make peace with the pope. In the picture, Alexander, with his foot on Barbarossa's neck, is extracting all he can from the papal victory.

When the Hohenstaufens gained power in the early 12th century, they were opposed by the Welfs, rival contenders for the imperial throne. One of the strongest of the Welfs was Heinrich the Lion, Duke of Saxony. Heinrich was married to Matilda (*above, left*), daughter of Henry II of England. (*Above, right*) The tomb of Heinrich the Lion and Matilda in the Cathedral of Brunswick, a town founded by Heinrich the Lion.

In 1172, Heinrich the Lion made a pilgrimage to the Holy Land. For much of the 11th and 12th centuries Christians had free access to Jerusalem, and were only in danger during times of open warfare between Christian and Moslem. (*Above*) Pilgrims kneel at their first sighting of Jerusalem. It was not unknown for Moslem leaders to supply pilgrims with guides and guards to protect them on their travels.

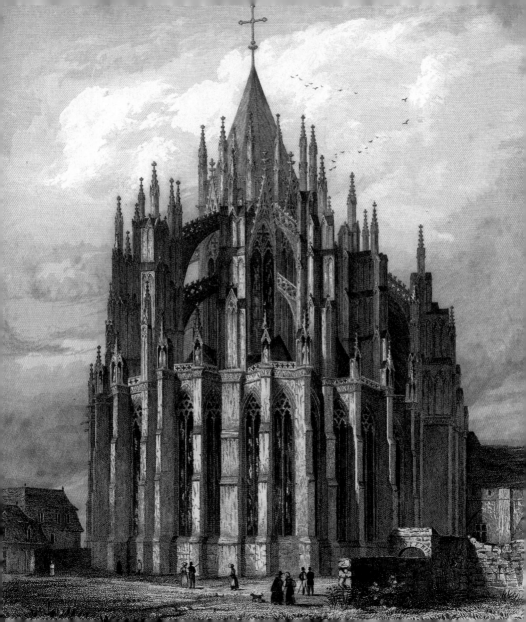

In 1181 what were taken to be the relics of the Three Wise Men, who had attended the birth of Christ, arrived in Cologne. The greatest goldsmith of the day, Nicholas de Verdun, was entrusted with the task of building a shrine to house these relics. This was the beginning of Cologne Cathedral (*opposite*), one of the mightiest ecclesiastical structures in Europe. It took over six hundred years to complete. (*Right*) Statuary lining the porch of Cologne Cathedral.

(*Left*) The monastery church at Murbach in Alsace, one of the finest achievements of late Salian architecture. The warm brown stone was imported from Burgundy, and the vast church has the weight and stature of a cathedral; indeed its whole design is remarkably similar to the old Salisbury Cathedral in England.

(*Right*) The nave of the Cathedral of St Maria in Basel, typical of the Salian architecture of the Upper Rhine. The cathedral was built with two enormous towers at the west end, tall enough almost to rival those of Strasbourg Cathedral. These buildings needed a vast amount of materials and a large workforce. The completion of such a structure was celebrated with much rejoicing, for it was seen as a tribute to God. It was also the object of much civic pride, though most of the workforce left as soon as it was finished to find another site where there were more plans to build to the glory of the Almighty.

The interiors of churches, chapels and cathedrals were often richly decorated. (*Right*) The interior of the apse of the Reichenau Church of SS Peter and Paul, Niederzell. As they knelt in prayer or stood to hear mass (for there were no pews or seats in 12th-century churches), the faithful were surrounded by images of Christ, the apostles, the martyrs and the saints. (*Opposite*) A religious painting by a Master of the Rhenish School in the 12th century. (Top left) the Fall of Man; (top right) the Annunciation; (bottom left) the Shepherds see the Star in the East; (bottom right) the Nativity.

3
THE WONDER
OF THE WORLD
1197–1250

Pillar capital in the former Benedictine monastery church of St
Michael, Hildesheim, Lower Saxony. By the 13th century, the
extent to which churches and cathedrals were decorated with
carvings and paintings had greatly increased. Many of the designs
in German ecclesiastical art owed much to Italian ideas, but in
Hildesheim there was already a tradition of sculpture – mainly
bronzework – dating back to Ottonian times in the 10th century.

Introduction

The old rivalries continued into the 13th century. On the death of Heinrich VI, the Hohenstaufens chose Philip, younger son of Barbarossa, as his successor. It seemed almost accepted that the imperial title was hereditary. However, the Welfs produced a rival candidate, Otto IV, who disposed of Philip by the simple means of having him murdered. Pope Innocent III then declared that only he had the right to select an emperor, and gave his support to Friedrich, Philip's younger brother.

Friedrich II was a strange character with forthright views. He told the pope that the three greatest swindlers in history were Moses, Jesus Christ and Mohammed, thus hardly endearing himself to the Holy Father, who already had doubts about the growing power of the Hohenstaufens in Italy.

It was said that Friedrich was the changeling son of a butcher, although his forty-year-old mother claimed that she had been delivered of her child under public scrutiny in the market-place at Jesi. After Friedrich's death in 1250 there were many who believed that he had not died, but was merely sleeping on a mountain top, and, like Arthur of England, was ready to return whenever his people had need of him. In other ways Friedrich was the first truly modern emperor, a figure who belonged more to the Renaissance than to the Middle Ages. He was a patron of the arts and sciences, a man of culture and learning, and the author of the definitive book on hunting with birds of prey – *De arte venandi cum avibus*. Sadly, he was also mean-minded, intolerant of the Jews, despotic and a vicious persecutor of heretics.

While Welfs and Hohenstaufens struggled for power, ordinary people struggled for a living. The first half of the 13th century saw further developments in medieval technology, a considerable increase in the number and efficiency of both wind- and water-mills, and the establishment of fine breweries – some of the best being in Essen and Dortmund. The German wine industry went from strength to strength. The Cistercian monks of Eberbach alone exported 53,000 gallons of wine a year down the River Rhine to Cologne.

Less intoxicating innovations included the arrival in Germany of the first camels, leopards and apes – brought back from the Holy Land by Friedrich II – and such domestic developments as the wheelbarrow, soap in hard cakes and the spiral staircase.

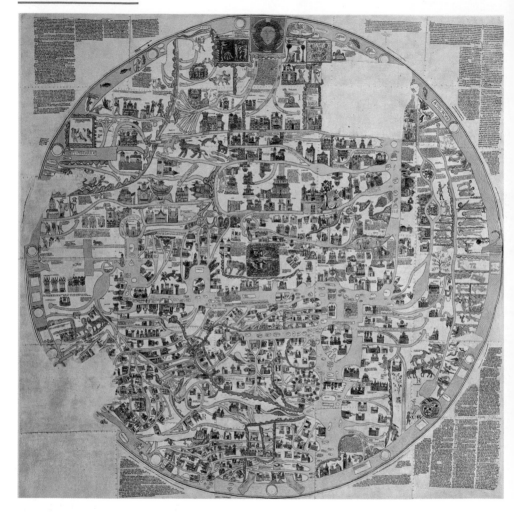

(*Above*) The Ebstorfer map of the world, from the late 13th century, with Jerusalem at its centre.
Housed in a monastery near the town of Velzen, northern Germany, it was made up of thirty manuscript
pages in parchment. This is a reconstruction: the original was burnt in a bombing raid in 1943.

(*Above, right*) A 13th-century drawing of the town of Tybur, with the River Aniene running through it. The town was situated in part of the imperial lands to the south of Rome. (*Below, right*) Leopold VI of Babenberg, Duke of Austria (centre, on horseback), rides in triumph into Vienna, 1219. Seven years earlier, he had led his troops in a Crusade against the Moors in Spain. Here, he had only recently returned from a Crusade to Palestine and Egypt. Leopold was an ardent and active supporter of the Emperor Friedrich II, and, for his ardent and active Christian zeal, was known as Leopold the Glorious.

Of all the early emperors, Friedrich II (*right*) was the most fascinating, the most outstanding and the most controversial. He was crowned King of Sicily at the age of two, and was only three when his father, Heinrich VI, died. He devoted his life to restoring the unity of the empire, and earned for himself the title *Stupor Mundi* – the Wonder of the World. His most lasting achievement, however, was his treatise on the art of hunting with birds – *De arte venandi cum avibus* (*opposite, above and below*).

In the centre of the city of Jerusalem (*above*) in the 13th century was the Holy German Hospital of St Mary. In times of peace it offered shelter and hospitality to pilgrims from all over the empire. In times of trouble, however, the Master of the Hospital and his followers were driven out, and had to find protection elsewhere. This was not always easy, for the peoples of the empire were not united in their views or allegiances.

Germans and Christians were at their most united when confronting a threat to the Holy Places. In the late 12th century, their most formidable opponent was Saladin (*above, left*), whose full title was Salah al-Din al-Ayyubi. Saladin captured Jerusalem in 1187 and spent the rest of his life fighting the Crusaders. Although remembered as a warrior, he was a wise administrator, an able builder of roads and canals, and a fair and pious man. (*Above, right*) A Crusader in a tower (with crossbow) faces besiegers armed with axes, catapults, hammers and longbows.

Friedrich II spent much of his reign seeking to strengthen his hold on northern Italy. 'He wanted to conquer the Lombards,' wrote Salimbe, a 13th-century chronicler, 'and could not... The men of Parma took his city, Vittoria, which he had built near Parma, and burned, razed, and completely destroyed it...his princes and barons rebelled against him...' (*Left*) The Castel del Monte in Apulia, built in 1233. Like many of Friedrich's castles, it was a combination stronghold and palace, virtually impregnable, but also offering a high level of comfort to its occupants.

(*Left*) The Mounted King on the first pillar of the north side of George's Choir, Bamberg Cathedral, known as the *Bamberger Reiter*. It was carved some time before 1237, and is almost 8 feet high. The cathedral itself was already some two hundred and fifty years old when this figure was installed. Equestrian statues like this are symbolic of the itinerant imperial court and of the emperor's concerns for his people. It is possible that this is an idealised portrait of Constantine the Great.

(*Right*) The Magdeburg Rider, in the Alter Markt. The figure dates from almost the same time as the Bamberg Rider, and is in many ways similar. In both sculptures the rider is seated firmly in the saddle, with his feet in the stirrups, his left hand grasping the reins of the horse. Both riders are beardless young men, wearing crowns. The Bamberg Rider, however, has no cloak. As in the case of the Bamberg Rider, no one knows for certain who the Magdeburg Rider is meant to represent.

These intricate and beautiful examples of German Romanesque sculpture come from a quartet of 12th-century churches. (*Above*) A cushion capital from the nave of the convent church of St Servatius, Quedlinburg, Saxony-Anhalt. (*Opposite, left*) A pillar of interwoven foliage and figures from the crypt of the Cathedral of St Mary, Freising, Bavaria. (*Opposite, above right*) Masks and dragons on the capital of the Hartmann column, church of SS Simon and Jude, Goslar, Lower Saxony. (*Opposite, below right*) Bearded mask and heads on a pillar capital in the nave of the Premonstratensian Church of St John the Baptist, Spieskappel, Hesse.

Two famous figures of the Middle Ages: (*left*) Doctor Universalis, whose real name was Albertus Magnus, a Dominican sage and writer. (*Opposite*) Doctor Angelicus, better known as St Thomas Aquinas, philosopher and theologian. Aquinas was also a member of the Dominican order. His teaching laid the foundations for much of modern Roman Catholic doctrine.

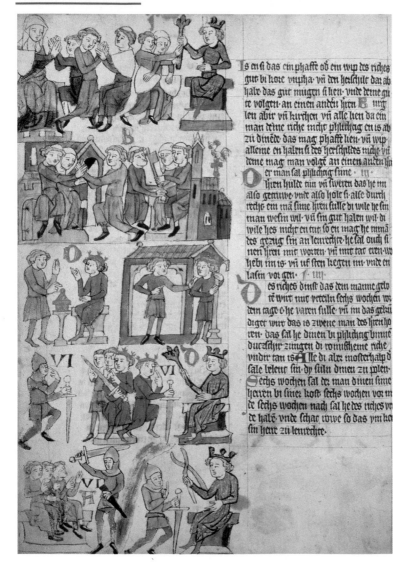

Is en si das em phaffe od em wip des riches gut bi kote vupha· vn den herschilt dar ab hale das gut muigen si lien· vnde deine gute volgten an einen andēn hren vrg lien abir vn kirschen vn alle lien da en man deine riche micht pfluchag en is ab zu dinēte das mag phaffe lien· vn wip allene en halen si des herschildes miche vn deme mag man volgte an einen andēn hin er man sal pfluchag sime · iij·

Yten hulde tin vn sweren das he in also getruwe vnde also hole si alse durch rechte en man sime hren sulle di wile he sin man wesin wil· vn sin gut halen wil· di wile hes micht en tut so en mag he nimā des gezug sin an lemrechte he sal ouch si nen hren mit worten vn mit tat eten· wo hebi tin is· vn uf sten tegen in· vnde en lasen vor gten· f· iiij·

es riches dinst das den manne gelo tt wirt nut pteiln sechs wochen vor dem tage o he varen sulle· vn in das gebiu diget wirt das is zwene man des hren ho ren· das sal he dinen bi pfluching vmut ducelschir zungen di romischene riche vndir tan is A lle di alre mosterhalp o sale teleum sin dp suln dinen zu polen· S echs wochen sal der man dinen sime herren bi siner kost sechs wochen vor m te sechs wochen nach sal he des riches vō te halb· vnde schar tiwe so das ym kei sin herre zu lemrechte·

(*Right*) Further examples of illustrations from the 14th century *Sachsenspiegel*. The scenes here represent the humdrum and the dramatic from everyday life, and provide a unique portrait of how people lived and what was considered important at this time.

In the early 13th century, German poetry reached a high point with the works of Walther von der Vogelweide and Wolfram von Eschenbach. Von der Vogelweide used his pen to praise a variety of imperial candidates. (*Left*) A portrait of Walther von der Vogelweide from the *Minnesänger, Codex Manesse*. The unknown artist has drawn von der Vogelweide in the very pose that the poet describes in the work itself.

(*Right*) A depiction of a scene from Wolfram von Eschenbach's *Parzival,* an epic that has for its theme the story of the Holy Grail, which was used as the inspiration for Wagner's opera. Wolfram also wrote seven *Love Songs,* a brief epic entitled *Willehalm* and two fragments called *Titurel.* The two poets are known to have met on at least one occasion at Wartburg Castle, home of the Landgrave of Thuringia.

In the west choir of the Cathedral of SS Peter and Paul at Naumburg are some of the most outstanding statues of 13th-century Europe. They are collectively called the Naumburg Benefactors, though the identity of every figure is not known. There are twelve figures in all. It is possible that they celebrate various citizens who responded to an appeal from Bishop Dietrich von Wettin for donations towards the cost of the cathedral. (*Opposite*) The Margrave Ekkehard and his wife Uta, representatives of the high nobility. (*Right*) An unidentified figure among the Naumburg Benefactors.

'Dear son, I will fit you out well and honourably…in such a manner as becomes a knightly man, so that you may exercise yourself in all knightly matters and tournaments, and be prepared to take your place among your equals and superiors who have been dubbed knights…' Extract from a letter to Jorg von Ehingen at the Court at Innsbruck, from his father.

Keeping up with one's alleged equals was an expensive business in medieval times. For a young man to take his turn at jousting (*opposite and above*), he required a horse, a page, armour, weapons, and considerable courage. Jousting was more than a sport. It was vital training in the techniques of fighting, and the lessons learned in the lists at tournaments might later save one's life on the battlefield.

bouure, ⁊ garder si de rourbles
⁊ de salees ⁊ dautres manieres
asses se ce nest por remouoir
maladies. mais se user les
estuet siles amendent selone
les ensegnemens que nous
desismes en le premiere partie.
car por les ensegnemens que
nous desismes feusismes la si nos
en passerons briement. de pui...

...ins si
se deu
sesie
en indi
tes ma
nieres
se sont
se sui...
...cauce
...selone
ce quil est nouuaus ⁊ vies ⁊
rour soir ce que routes manie...
...va de sun eseausur salene...

Although the Church imposed strict rules governing eating and drinking, the citizens of the empire were quick to enjoy both when the harvest and their purses permitted. (*Above, left*) Picking grapes and operating a wine press some time in the 11th century. (*Below, left*) Two classes of dinner. The cloth, the utensils and the bowls in the upper half of the picture all suggest that this is a well-to-do family. The lower picture is of a banquet in a noble household, with minstrels present and servants waiting at table.

The noble art of guzzling. (*Opposite, below right*) A monk sips from a bowl of wine. The expression on his face could indicate that this is an unofficial visit to the cellar. The wine pouring from the cask into a jug indicates that it could also be a prolonged visit. (*Right*) A busy night in a tavern. Again, the picture is divided into two halves. In the top half there are people enjoying tankards and flasks of beer or wine. In the bottom half the landlord draws more supplies from the depths of his cellar.

Throughout the 12th and 13th centuries life on the land was harsh. Oxen were cumbersome draught animals (*above*) and ploughing took up many hard and exhausting hours. Breaking up the clods of earth and weeding was all done by hand. (*Left*) A 12th-century picture of a pair of angels blessing shepherds and their flock. 'Each shepherd must cover his fold and enclose it with hurdles and mend it...and he ought to sleep in the fold, he and his dog...' – extract from a 13th-century account of the duties of a shepherd.

Among the most successful farmers and agriculturists of the 13th century were the Cistercian monks. They were pioneers in good husbandry, and possessed the most advanced technology. (*Above*) Cistercian monks ploughing the fields attached to their monastery, with a neat garden in the background. (*Right*) An illuminated letter from a 13th-century manuscript showing the various farming activities of a group of monks.

4
BIRTH PANGS
1250–1350

The steady rise in population during the late 13th and early 14th centuries led to the growth of many German towns. Food became more plentiful. The transport of goods by road and river became easier. Capital was more readily available for new entrepreneurs. Towns in southern Germany tended to be centres for craftsmen, organised into guilds. In the north, towns were populated more by merchants and traders. Civic pride led to rivalry between towns in building the finest churches, town and guild halls, and houses. This town (*right*) is Horb am Neckar, with the parish church (centre) and the 'Rogue's Tower' (left).

Introduction

That the empire should have survived at all during this period seems something of a miracle. For the best part of a hundred years it was torn apart by internal strife, by rival candidates, by a debilitating involvement in Italian politics, and by hostility to and from the papacy.

Schiller labelled the mid-13th century ' a terrible time without an emperor', but more often through the 13th and 14th centuries there were too many emperors. Rudolf of Habsburg did what he could to secure his hold on the imperial throne, and secure an unopposed succession after his death, by arranging a series of marriages. He married his four daughters respectively to the Duke of Bavaria, the Duke of Saxony, the King of Hungary and the King of Bohemia. Having done that, he turned to older ways, bringing order to Thuringia by destroying more than fifty castles, which he saw as centres of opposition.

Weddings and destruction did little to bring stability to the empire. When Rudolf died his son Albrecht's succession was challenged by Adolf of Nassau, until the latter was killed at the Battle of Gollheim in 1298. Ten years later, Albrecht himself was murdered by his disaffected nephew Johannes. The new emperor, Heinrich VII, ventured into Italy, where he was welcomed by Dante, championed by the Ghibelline faction, and shot at by the rival Guelphs. While this was going on, the security of the empire was not improved by the removal of the papal court to Avignon, where popes remained under French control for over a hundred years.

Following Heinrich VII's death, Duke Friedrich the Fair of Austria was elected emperor on 19 September 1314. The following day Ludwig of Upper Bavaria was also elected to the same throne. For eight years both avoided a test of strength to determine who should rule, but in 1322 Ludwig emerged victorious from the Battle of Mühldorf.

It did him little good. Ludwig was excommunicated by the octogenarian Pope John XXII, and shortly afterwards died of a stroke while out bear-hunting. The intricate nonsense that bedevilled the cause of the empire came to an end with the election of Karl IV in 1347. Karl kept out of Italian politics, and cemented his position by building up a dynastic empire based on his hereditary domains of Bohemia and Moravia.

Even for those with the good sense or good luck to stand apart from these absurdities, the age was one of appalling natural disasters. Three years of devastating famine from 1315 were followed by earthquakes and swarms of locusts. Then, in 1351, came the Black Death. In their terror, many blamed the Jews.

The Hohenstaufen ruling dynasty came to an end with the death of Konrad IV in 1254. His son, Konradin of Swabia (*above*), had a legitimate claim to the kingdom of Naples and Sicily, but was opposed by Charles of Anjou, who had the support of Pope Urban IV. Konradin challenged Charles's claim, and took up arms, but was defeated and captured. He was beheaded on 28 October 1268 (*left*). His body was dismembered, and pieces of his flesh passed to the watching crowd.

Rudolf I (*left*) was the first of the Habsburg emperors. His coronation marked the end of the 'terrible time without an emperor' for Germany. Although fifty-five years old when he became emperor in 1273 (old by the standards of the age), Rudolf fought hard and successfully to assert his authority. The fight took its toll. In 1291, while journeying to Speyer (*above*), Rudolf died at Germersheim.

On Rudolf's death, Adolf of Nassau was elected emperor. At the behest of the Archbishop of Mainz and the King of Bohemia, however, Adolf was deposed and Albrecht I, son of Rudolf (*above, left*), took his place. Adolf was defeated and killed at the Battle of Gollheim in 1298. Hartman of Habsburg (*above, right*) was Rudolf's third son. He was drowned in the Rhine on 21 December 1282, at the age of nineteen.

The machinations of rival factions to secure the election of whichever candidate they supported as emperor continued into the 14th century. When Albrecht I died in 1306 there were two candidates – Charles of Valois, and Heinrich of Luxemburg. The diplomatic skills of the Archbishop of Trier led to the defeat of Charles and the election of Heinrich VII (*opposite*). (*Above*) Heinrich VII receives a deputation from Jewish merchants.

Leopold of Habsburg, Duke of Austria and Styria (*above, left*), was the third son of the Emperor Albrecht I. Like Albrecht II, Leopold spent most of his adult life attempting to suppress the Swiss struggle for independence, led by William Tell (*above, right*). There is much doubt that Tell ever existed, but the legends persist. It is said that he refused to do reverence to the ducal hat, placed on a pole in his home town of Bürglen, and as a test of his skill (and self-confidence) was forced to shoot an apple from his son's head (*opposite, below*).

Leopold led an Austrian army into the Swiss cantons to put an end to the rebellion. On 13 November 1315, his army was routed at the Battle of Morgarten (*right*), where Swiss troops hurled rocks and tree trunks down on the invading Austrians.

The Swiss fight for freedom continued for another seventy-one years after the Battle of Morgarten. On 9 July 1386, the decisive battle took place by the lakeside at Sempach, in the canton of Lucerne (*above*). The Austrians suffered a crushing defeat, their heavily armed knights being no match for the Swiss pikemen. Duke Leopold III of Austria was among those killed.

THANENFLL

NOTPWIL

HANS VON ROT

DER SEE

KILPEL

OBER
KILCH

Schwäbisch Hall (*left, above and below*) was built near salt springs. It was also an important centre of minting, making the silver *Haller*, the smallest unit of currency in the Holy Roman Empire. 'Nothing more magnificent or splendid is to be found in the whole of Europe,' wrote Pope Pius II of the medieval town of Nuremberg (*opposite*). 'The burghers' dwellings seem to have been built for princes. In truth, the kings of Scotland would be glad to be housed so luxuriously as the ordinary citizen of Nuremberg...'

In 1254 a group of Rhenish towns formed the League of the Rhine, which eventually grew to include trading centres from Lübeck to Zurich. At the height of its influence, the League claimed the right to rule Germany pending the election of a suitable king. Three important members of the League: (*right*) Mainz, (*opposite, above*) Worms, (*opposite, below*) Bacharach.

The most commercially powerful of the German trading associations was the Hanseatic League. The League consisted of over one hundred and fifty towns, joined together for trade and mutual protection. Hamburg was one of the principal members. (*Opposite*) An illustration from the Hamburg municipal by-laws, showing merchants and sailors in Hamburg harbour. (*Above*) The seals of eight members of the Hanseatic League: Lübeck, Wismar, Rostock, Stralsund, Greifswald, Stettin, Kolberg and Anklam. The document refers to their union against the Danish king and the pirates who operated in the Baltic.

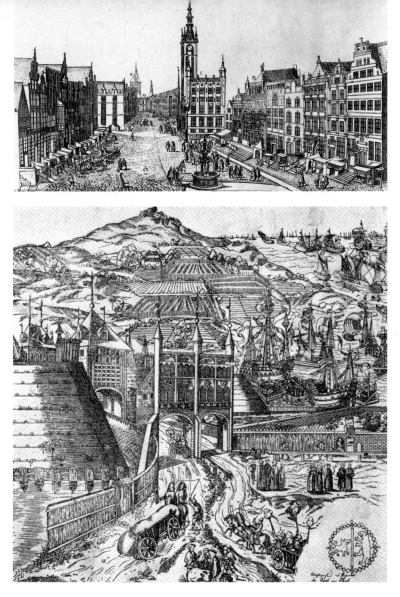

(*Opposite*) Hans Holbein's portrait of a German merchant who was a member of the Hanseatic League. (*Above, right*) The centre of Danzig in the heyday of the Hanseatic League. (*Below, right*) Ships fill the busy harbour of Lübeck, while a procession of carts enters through the town gates. The League flourished for well over two hundred years, dominating the east–west trade from the Atlantic to the Baltic. Eventually, the rise of the nation state in north-east Europe challenged and finally took away the League's privileges.

ces portes restraingnent le si
Li xij. cap dou purgien

pres
che q
dir v
awns
dou sai
nier si
vould
rons
comen
on dir

te cors purgier: car cest vne co

Medical science was still very much a hit-and-miss affair in medieval Germany. Old remedies were still applied and old beliefs still practised in rural areas, but newer and more sophisticated methods of treatment existed in towns and cities. A 14th-century treatise on medicine placed obligations on patients as well as surgeons. 'The conditions required of a sick man are three: that he be obedient to the doctor...; that he have faith in the doctor...; that he be patient, for patience conquers malice...' (*Left*) A doctor administers a potion to a patient, c. 1400.

One of the commonest forms of treatment was bleeding, relieving the patient of the bad humours that caused illness or disease. (*Right*) A medieval doctor bleeds a patient's arm, and collects the blood in a vessel, c. 1350. (*Below, and opposite, below*) Six illustrations from a medieval manuscript on surgery, showing various ways in which to set a broken arm. Although some of the techniques may appear rough-and-ready, they were a considerable advance on earlier methods.

No European country escaped the Black Death. This virulent outbreak of plague struck Germany in 1348, killing between one-third and one-half of the population in many areas. Nobody knew what caused the plague; many had theories. It was blamed on 'bad air', or poisoned water. A Dominican monk named Heinrich von Herford reported that many Jews in Germany were put to death 'in the most horrible and inhuman manner, by iron and fire', though he personally did not believe that they were responsible for the epidemic. (*Above*) The effect of the plague in Basle, 1349.

Some were certain they knew the cause – sin. Not until people had purged themselves of the evil within would God relent and the plague go away. And the best way to drive out the evil was by self-flagellation. Processions of flagellants passed through many German towns and villages (*above*). These processions were often headed by a priest, and were preceded by the rabidly devout carrying banners and a crucifix. The Church disapproved, claiming it alone had the right to decide how sins were to be forgiven or expiated. A Papal Bull of 1349 declared that flagellants were heretics.

Illness, famine and most natural disasters were seen as either the work of God, or of God's enemies. In the fiercely Christian society of medieval Germany, the Jews were repeatedly seen as undeservedly wealthy and wickedly cunning. (*Above*) An illustration from the *Liber Chronicarum Mundi* of Nuremberg, showing Jews being burnt alive in Cologne in 1493. (*Opposite*) A 14th-century depiction of a scene from the Book of Revelation, showing a holy figure (possibly St Peter), an enchained figure of evil, and three men standing in an animal's mouth.

po
ka
lyp
sis
dit
ist
die
offe
barunge ihesu cristi. Die
yme goth gegebin hat
offenbar zcu tune sine
knechten die schire ge
schen sal.

The *Manesse Codex* of the early 14th century was a collection of the medieval songs of well over a hundred German poets, collected by Rüdiger Manesse. The songs were based on love poems that graphically portrayed the pains and pleasures of love itself. (*Left*) *Kosendes Paar* – a young couple find time to embrace each other in a moment of calm and seclusion. (*Opposite*) A knight and his love flee from their pursuers. Both illustrations are from the *Manesse Codex*.

(*Left*) A further illustration from the *Manesse Codex*, depicting a young German gentleman taking a bath. The scene is titillatingly idyllic. The man is surrounded by young maidens who anoint him with oil, warm the water for his bath, and sprinkle his body with the petals of flowers.

Othon,
Marquis de Brandebourg,
jouant aux Echécs.

Bibliot.ᵉ du Roi.

Willemin del. et sculp.ᵗ

(*Above*) Otto, Margrave of Brandenburg, and his wife enjoy a game of chess, c. 1350. The game arrived in Spain and Italy from Persia at the beginning of the second Christian millennium, but took another two hundred years to reach Germany. It was well established throughout Europe by 1400, with the same rules and the same pieces that are used today.

Karl IV of Luxemburg (*opposite, below*) became Holy Roman Emperor in 1355, at the age of thirty-nine. He spent much of his early life in Prague (*right*), the capital of Bohemia, and a safe refuge from his rivals. Prague became an increasingly important city. It was created an archbishopric in 1344 and its university was founded in 1348. The magnificent Karl Bridge over the River Moldau is witness to the importance Karl attached to the city. (*Opposite, above*) The meeting between Karl IV and Charles V of France, 1370. Charles regained much of France from Edward III of England, who had been Karl's rival as emperor in 1355.

La venue de lempere? charles
en france et de sa receptió
par le roy charles le quint.

Karl IV also did much to enhance the glory and the beauty of Nuremberg during his twenty-two-year reign. He visited the city more than fifty times, and contributed to the construction of the Frauenkirche (*left and opposite*) on the east side of the Hauptmarkt. The church became the emperor's court chapel, and was one of the first masterpieces of Peter Parler, the young architect from Schwäbisch-Gmund.

When it was completed in the 14th century, Strasbourg Cathedral (*left and opposite*) was not only the tallest – its spire reached 466 feet in height – but was considered the most beautiful building in the world, and, indeed, the very centre of Christendom. Inside and out, it was a magnificent achievement, a triumph of the architectural and engineering skills of medieval times.

The initial design was the work of Erwin von Steinbach, and work on the cathedral began in 1250. The west façade (*right*) dates from 1277, but the building was not finished until 1320. Not the least of its many astounding features is the spiral staircase, which climbs through the octagon of the cathedral to a height of 108 feet.

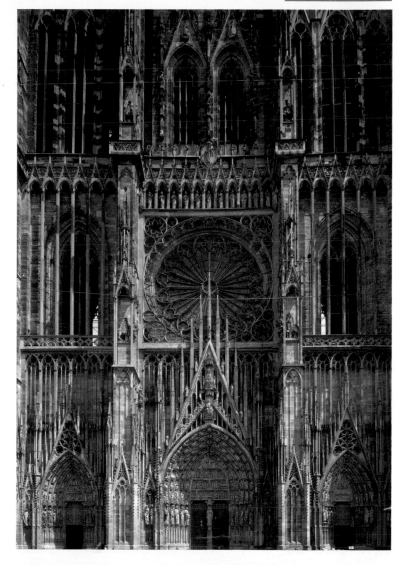

5

BOHEMIAN HERESY
1350–1438

Jan Hus is burnt at the stake in the public square at Konstanz, 6 July 1415. He had been promised safe conduct by the Emperor Sigismund, but was seized and thrown into prison. At his trial Hus was neither allowed to speak freely in his defence, nor to appoint a defender. Hus was a peasant's son who became a priest, a preacher and a professor at Prague University. His crime, known as the Bohemian heresy, was that he acknowledged Christ, and not the pope, as head of the Church. His death sparked off a brutal religious war, in which his own followers did little to honour his memory.

Introduction

The divisions within the empire continued. There were times when there were three emperors, times when there were three popes. The Golden Bull of Nuremberg, issued in 1356, attempted to rationalise imperial elections. In future there were to be just seven appointed electors. But the efficacy of this system, and indeed the fortunes of the empire, were inextricably linked to the strength of any imperial candidate. When the preferred candidate was strong, the election went smoothly ahead and the empire itself was strong. When the candidate was weak, he was invariably opposed by other candidates and the empire suffered yet another of its regular periods of turmoil.

Emperor Sigismund, the younger son of Karl IV, had much of his father's spirit. He championed Christian civilisation against the Turks, and presided effectively over the Council of Constance, itself a mixed blessing. On the positive side, it ended the Great Schism – the existence of two popes, one at Avignon, one in Rome. Like the empire, the Church was at the mercy of its own head – and the popes were a mixed bunch at this time – but after Constance it was nominally united.

The Council was less praiseworthy for its treatment of Jan Hus. Hus was a professor at Prague University, and a follower of the teachings of the English religious reformer, John Wycliffe. Suspected of heresy, Hus was excommunicated. He lost the backing of the university, but found much support among the nobles. In 1414 he was summoned to the Council of Constance. Sigismund guaranteed him safe conduct, but when Hus arrived he was thrown into prison. His trial was a travesty, and Hus was publicly burnt at the stake on 6 July 1415. His followers were enraged, and a lengthy and bloody war broke out in Bohemia, seriously weakening the empire.

Rivalry between the princes deepened. Separate capitals were established in Munich, Prague and Graz, the centre of the empire constantly shifting. A similar rivalry existed between the newly established universities (Prague, Vienna, Heidelberg, Cologne and Leipzig), each seeking to seduce the others' scholars. Finance teetered on the brink of the modern world. Local rulers supplemented their traditional sources of income – from customs dues and coin-minting – by raising taxes. And in South Germany, the Fugger family began to amass the fortune on which their later banking empire was to be founded.

The most inventive mind of the age was that of Konrad Kyeser. He was born at Eichstätt in 1366, and was a Bavarian forerunner of Leonardo da Vinci. Kyeser designed floating and folding bridges, assault towers, armoured vehicles, diving suits and diving helmets, and an early form of the revolver.

Karl IV spent only one day in Italy, where he was crowned emperor in 1355, before hastily returning to Germany. The following year, at the Assembly of Nuremberg, it was agreed that in future the seven imperial electors should be the King of Bohemia, the Archbishops of Mainz, Trier and Cologne, the Elector Palatine, the Duke of Saxony and the Margrave of Brandenburg. This agreement was subsequently published as the Golden Bull of 1356, as the seal attached to the document was made of gold, not wax. (*Opposite*) Karl IV (emperor and King of Bohemia) with the three spiritual and three temporal electors. (*Above*) Karl IV rides with the three temporal electors (carrying banners) and the Archbishop of Trier.

(*Left*) The spires of the old town of Prague, with the statues that line the Karl Bridge in the foreground. (*Below, left*) Karl's son Wenzel, a brutal and headstrong man whose reign as emperor from 1378 to 1400 was not a success. He failed to end the struggle for power between the towns and the princes, and was deposed by the German electors.

(Opposite, below right)
Ruprecht of the Palat-
inate, who succeeded
Wenzel as emperor from
1400 to 1410. He
founded the University of
Heidelberg as an intellectual power base for Rome,
but failed to heal the
papal schism between
Avignon and Rome.
(Right) The 14th-century
Cathedral of Notre Dame
de Tyn in Prague, with
part of Prague Castle in
the background.

The wars that raged throughout central Europe in the 14th and 15th centuries were brutal in their execution, but were usually preceded by a strictly enforced ceremonial summoning rival armies to battle. (*Above*) An engraving from the *Kriegsbuch* of Frankfurt showing a herald calling on the inhabitants of a besieged city to open the gates and throw down their arms.

(*Top*) An early 15th-century illustration of the different classes of warrior armed for battle. On the left are the pikemen, wearing little or no armour. In the centre are the knights, also carrying pikes, but armed with swords and protected by plate armour or chainmail. On the right are the electors and emperors, protected from head to toe, and with flowing plumes on their helmets. (*Above*) A mounted band precedes the arrival of a group of knights at a late medieval tournament.

(*Left*) The 15th-century
Cathedral of Konstanz in
south-west Germany. In
1417 the Council of
Konstanz ended the Great
Schism in the Catholic
Church. Pope John XXII
and Pope Benedict XIII of
Avignon were deposed.
The Roman pope,
Gregory XII, resigned.
The Council was largely
the work of the Emperor
Sigismund (*opposite,
above left*), younger son of
Karl IV, and one of the
few emperors whose
imperial claim was
unchallenged.

The new pope was
Martin V (*above, right*),
who presided over the
remaining sessions of the
Council (*below, left and
right*). Although
Sigismund had promised
to protect Jan Hus, it was
the Council of Konstanz
that condemned the
Bohemian preacher and
sentenced him to death.
Their vain hope was that
this would put an end to
the Bohemian heresy.
Within twenty years,
however, the Council and
the papacy were engaged
in a mutually destructive
power struggle.

Part of the challenge that Jan Hus presented to the Church came from the power and nature of his preaching. Not only were his views on the papacy itself unacceptable, Hus followed some of the teachings of the English preacher John Wycliffe, advocating the translation of the Bible into the vernacular. (*Above, left*) Hus preaches to some of his followers, c. 1410. (*Below, left*) Emperor Sigismund signs the death warrant of Jan Hus.

Even in his prison cell, Hus was unrepentant and continued preaching (*above, right*). His execution (*below, right*) was seen by his supporters as the seal of the truth of his doctrines, and he became an instant martyr. In many ways, the duplicity of the Church and the emperor in their treatment of Hus prepared the way for Martin Luther and the far greater challenge that the Catholic Church was to face a hundred years later.

Work began on the magnificent Münster at Ulm (*above*) in Baden-Württemberg towards the end of the 14th century. The master mason was Heinrich Parler of Cologne, father of Peter Parler who built the Frauenkirche in Nuremberg. It was designed as a parish church, but with a capacity to hold a congregation of 20,000 – more than twice the contemporary population of Ulm, then one of the largest cities in Germany.

The spire remained unfinished for more than four hundred years. Cracks had begun to appear in the masonry and it was not until the late 19th century that a way was found to support the spire. (*Right*) The west front of the Münster at Ulm, decorated with scenes from the Book of Genesis and statues of saints carved by Master Hartmann.

The late 14th and early 15th centuries saw the establishment of several new universities in Germany and the empire. In some cases there were political reasons behind the foundations, but there was also a genuine desire to increase and disseminate new learning. (*Left*) A lecturer and his students at Strasbourg University, late 15th century. (*Opposite*) The Great Hall of the University of Heidelberg, during a lecture.

Hohe Schul zu Heydelberg.

Johannes Fugger was a master weaver who settled in Augsburg in 1368. His second son, Jakob Fugger (*opposite, right*), built on the business, and the Fugger family became immensely wealthy, branching out to own almost all the mines and metal works in Hungary. Jakob was nicknamed 'the Rich', and emperors and princes flocked to him, to plead for loans and credit. The emperors Maximilian and Karl V granted the family a virtual monopoly over the production of silver, copper and mercury throughout the Habsburg lands.

The foundation of the Fugger fortune: (*opposite*) Hans Burgkmair's illustration of a cloth merchant in his storehouse. (*Above, left*) A contemporary woodcut of another merchant's shop. The Fugger family granted Karl V a loan of more than 500,000 guilders for his imperial election campaign in 1519 – at a time when a schoolteacher earned less than four guilders a year.

Jakob Fugger II (*below, left*) was the first modern business tycoon. (*Left*) the city of Augsburg, home of the Fugger family. (*Below, right*) The emblem of the Fugger family, worked into the façade of a medieval house in Augsburg. (*Opposite*) *An Allegory of Trade* by Jost Amman, from his collection of woodcuts recording the lives of merchants in German history. The merchant himself is to be seen on the raised dais, to the top of the picture.

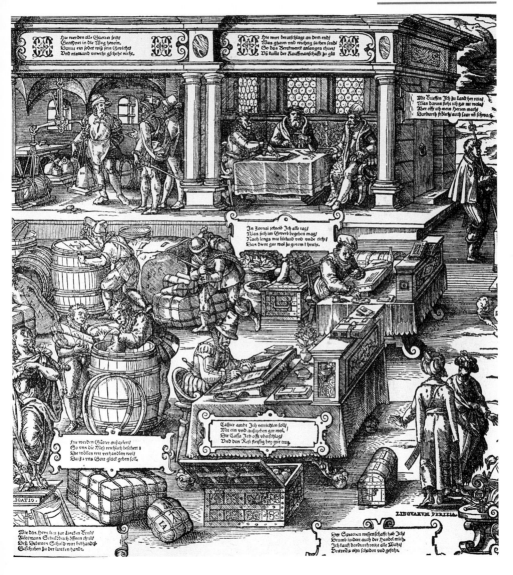

Good works were much praised by the Church, and ensured the men and women responsible for them were remembered and commemorated after their deaths. The paths to Heaven and Hell were clearly defined in medieval society. (*Left*) Friedrich I, Elector of Brandenburg, at prayer c. 1400. Piety and devotion were publicly displayed by all from the humblest to the highest.

(*Above, right*) A friar preaches from a movable pulpit to an open-air congregation. The quality of such preaching varied enormously, from the galvanising to the soporific. (*Below, left*) A medieval depiction of St Christopher, the 3rd-century Christian martyr who became the patron saint of travellers. (*Below, right*) Ministering angels attend the bedside of a sick man. Their strength and compassion, and the self-sacrificial nature of their work, drives the devil (emerging from under the bed) to fury.

But just as there were angels within society, so also there were devils. (*Above*) A full-page woodcut from the *Passio Jesu Christi*, with accompanying German text. Devils and friends gather round the bedside of a dying man. The gleeful expressions on the faces of the devils suggest that the poor man's life after death will not be a happy one. The glum expressions on the faces of his friends suggest that they will later be joining him.

Satan was regularly abroad in the 14th and 15th centuries – tempting, destroying, entering the souls of the damned. And if Satan himself was too busy, he would send his minions. (*Above*) A witch, a demon and a warlock descend upon a poor peasant woman – from a woodcut in a chapbook of the early 15th century.

(*Left*) A wealthy prince dines at his table, late 15th century. Titbits from the feast are offered to the prince's hawk and to his dogs. While the priest blesses the food on the table, servants wait to bring in a further selection of dishes.
(*Opposite, above*) The dining-room in the house of a rich merchant.
(*Opposite, below*) Eight peasants enjoy an open-air meal in the village of Mogeldorf; one does not.

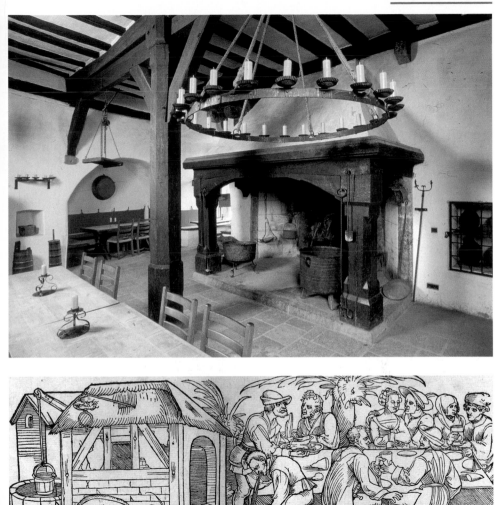

6
THE LAST KNIGHT
1438–1519

The single most important invention of the Middle Ages. (*Right*)
Johannes Gensfleisch Gutenberg examines a page from the first
printing press to employ a movable metal type, Mainz, c. 1450.
The two hundred and ninety-six typefaces, based on contemporary calligraphy, were cast from a mixture of lead, antimony,
bismuth and tin, and stored in a specially made case with the
most frequently used letters most readily to hand. In the
following fifty years over 5 million printed books were produced,
revolutionising the spread of learning.

Introduction

In 1453 two events changed the course of European history: the Turks captured Constantinople, and Johannes Gutenberg of Mainz produced his forty-two-line edition of the Bible using movable type.

The Emperor Friedrich III turned his back on the first event, and, like most Germans, little realised the profound effect the second was to have on the subsequent development of the empire. For the present, much of Germany was more involved in the customary round of civil wars – between the estates and the Teutonic Knights, between Hungary and Emperor Friedrich III, between Charles the Bold of Burgundy and the Swiss, and between Charles and Friedrich. When all this fighting came to an end with the proclamation of Perpetual Peace at the Diet of Worms in 1495, one thing was certain: militarily speaking, the days of the knight-at-arms were over.

Where and while there was peace, German

culture flourished. Artistically, it was the age of Dürer, Cranach and Bernard. Musically, there was the first flowering of German song, the old folk modes gradually giving way to a richer choral sound. The goldsmiths of Germany were the finest in Europe. Architecture literally reached new heights with the completion of St Martin Tower, Landshut, the domes of the Frauenkirche, Munich, and Bremen Cathedral – as well as many fine town and guild halls.

Thomas Hamerken of Kempen (better known in the West as Thomas à Kempis) published his inspirational *On the Following* (or *Imitation*) *of Christ.* Johann Sprenger and Heinrich (Institoris) Kraemer wrote their *Malleus Maleficarum,* handbook on conducting the trials of witches. Anton Koburger of Nuremberg published Latin and German versions of Hartmann Schedel's *World Chronicle.* In 1505 *Rerum Germanicarum* appeared, the first history of Germany.

After all the death and suffering caused by the 14th-century plagues, hygiene made great advances in medieval Germany. Bath-houses were established in most towns (though their use was at times controversial); people took far greater care of their hair, their skin and their teeth; and shaving lost much of its rudimentary blood-letting.

On the land, life was still harsh. Almost every year a peasants' revolt (*Bundschuh*) broke out somewhere in Germany during the late 15th and early 16th centuries – notably at Allgäu in 1492, in Alsace the following year, in Spires in 1502 and in Breisgau in 1513. Little was done to alleviate the suffering of the poor. In 1519, under the sponsorship of the great banking family, settlements for the homeless (*Fuggerei*) were established in Augsburg, but much more was needed.

Perhaps more significantly, in view of what was to come, in 1519 the Fuggers secured the right to sell indulgences throughout Germany.

Gutenberg borrowed 1,750 guilders from Johann Fust to set up his first printing press and produce copies of his first printed work, the Bible. Five years later, Fust demanded his money back, and Gutenberg became bankrupt. Gutenberg later resumed work on a more modest scale, producing a Psalter in 1457 and a Latin dictionary three years later. Eventually, Gutenberg received a pension from Adolf of Nassau.

(*Above, left*) Sebastian Brant, a German poet who was born in Strasbourg. Brant's most famous work was *The Ship of Fools* (*Narrenschiff*), a satire on the vices and follies of his times, first published in 1494. The poetry within the work was not of the highest quality, but the book contained much common sense and good moral teaching. Brant was also a lecturer at Basle University. (*Above, right*) A pair of illustrations from *The Ship of Fools*, from the original edition.

ALBERTVS·MI·DI·SA·SANC·
ROMANAE·ECCLAE·TI·SAN·
CHRYSOGONI·PBR·CARDINA·
MAGVN·AC·MAGDE·ARCHI·
EPS·ELECTOR·IMPE·PRIMAS·
ADMINI·HALBER·MAR·CHI·
BRANDENBVRGENSIS·

(*Left*) An illustration from Hartman Schedel's *Liber Chronicarum*, with woodcuts and drawings by Michael Wolgemut and Wilhelm Pleyenwurff, produced in Nuremberg in 1493. The illustration depicts the political structure of the empire. In the top row, the seven electors pay court to the emperor himself. Below them are some of the princes of the Holy Roman Empire, bearing their coats of arms. (*Above*) A man of power, piety and influence: Cardinal Albrecht, Archbishop of Mainz and Magdeburg, and Elector of the Holy Roman Empire, c. 1520. He was given special dispensation to hold two dioceses by Pope Leo X after contributing to the fund to rebuild St Peter's in Rome.

Friedrich III (*left*) was unanimously elected to the imperial throne in 1439, and remained emperor for the next fifty-three years. He did not have an easy reign. In 1453 Constantinople, long the eastern outpost of Christendom, fell to the Turks. Friedrich decided that his principal duty was not to protect Bohemia or Hungary, but to concentrate on the western domains of the empire.

(*Below, left*) The Empress Leonore, wife of Friedrich III. (*Below, right*) Matthias Corvinus, King of Hungary from 1458 to 1490. Corvinus had to struggle for more than six years to secure his throne against the Turks, the Bohemians and disaffected local magnates. Having done that, his next task was to attack Friedrich. In 1485 Matthias besieged and captured Vienna (*right*).

Maximilian I (*above, left*), who succeeded Friedrich III, was known as the Last Knight. He was a military and political reformer, who realised that the days of the Teutonic knight were strategically over, that in future battles would be decided by the Landsknecht and artillery. (*Above, right*) Margaret of Austria, daughter of Maximilian, queen regent of the Netherlands and guardian of her nephew, the future Emperor Karl V. (*Opposite*) *The Wheel of State*, as depicted in a woodcut by Hans Burgkmair.

Burgkmair was a prolific artist. Among his seven hundred woodcuts was a series of scenes depicting the life of Maximilian. (*Left*) Maximilian attends High Mass. (*Opposite*) *Stolen Cattle are Reclaimed from the Rebels of 1485* – another scene from the life of Maximilian. Widespread revolt broke out in Utrecht in 1484 during the war in the Netherlands, and was fiercely crushed by the emperor.

On 29 August 1526, Ludwig II of Hungary (*opposite*) was defeated and killed by the Turks under Suleiman the Magnificent at the Battle of Mohacs (*above, right*). The defeat was a turning-point in German history, for Austria, Hungary and Bohemia now became united and passed into the hands of the Habsburg dynasty. (*Right, below*) A contemporary drawing showing five men in ornate Hungarian dress, carrying substantial sheilds and heavy iron clubs, none of which seems to have frightened the Turks at Mohacs.

A glorious example of Flemish religious painting in the late 15th century – Hans Memling's triptych of *The Virgin and Child with Saints and Doctors,* c. 1470 – main panel (*above*) and side panels (*opposite*). Memling was born in Seligenstadt on the River Main some time between 1435 and 1440. As a young man he went to Brussels and then Bruges, where he studied as a painter under Rogier van der Weyden. Some of the many delights to be found in the works of Memling are the detailed landscape backgrounds to his religious paintings.

The Landsknecht were the troops of German mercenary soldiers, mainly pikemen, who replaced the mounted knights of the old age of chivalry as the main strike force in 16th-century warfare. (*Above*) Fierce combat between groups of pikemen. (*Far left*) A poorly mounted medieval German warrior. (*Left*) A stocky member of the Landsknecht.

Portraits of four German mercenaries by an unknown artist of the mid-16th century. The weapons they carried were not standard, though most carried a pike. In many cases, these professional soldiers bought their own swords and early firearms, or picked them up from the dead on the field of battle. The almost constant state of war within the scattered domains of the empire ensured that they were seldom short of work.

The noisy, smoky and terrifying new weapon on the battlefield was the cannon. Its effect was largely theatrical at first, but by the mid-16th century artillery pieces were as important militarily as the cavalry and infantry. (*Opposite*) Emperor Maximilian consults with craftsmen in a cannon foundry, c. 1550. (*Above*) Hans Burgkmair's engraving of soldiers loading artillery pieces before a battle.

The greatest German artist of the late 15th and early 16th centuries was Albrecht Dürer (*opposite*), born in Nuremberg in 1471. His father, Albrecht Dürer senior (*above, left*), was a goldsmith from Hungary. At the age of fifteen, Dürer was apprenticed to Michael Wolgemut, the chief illustrator of the *Nuremberg Chronicle.* Nine years later he began working independently as an artist. (*Above, right*) Dürer's portrait of his mother. The inscription reads: 'That is Albrecht Dürer's mother; she was 63 years old. She died in the year 1514 on the Tuesday before Rogation week about two hours before night.'

Although Dürer executed many great paintings – including his *Adoration of the Magi* (*right*) – he is perhaps best remembered for his extraordinary ability as a draughtsman and engraver. (*Opposite*) Dürer's study of a late medieval knight. (*Below, left*) *The Study for the Hands of an Apostle*, c. 1508. (*Below, right*) Draft for a woodcut illustrating the proportions of the human body. The sketch is of an ageing woman, and includes many corrections.

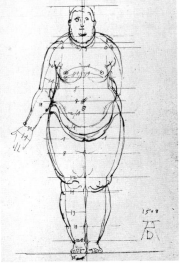

(*Left*) Mounted trumpeters and kettle drummers from the imperial army, an example from a highly detailed and exquisitely executed series of woodcuts by Hans Burgkmair. By the early 16th century kings and emperors were not only political and military rivals, but also rivals as showmen. Henry VIII of England, Francis I of France and the Emperor Karl V all sought to provide the most lavish display of wealth.

(*Right*) A detail from the magnificently carved altarpiece in the church of St Jakob, Rothenburg ob der Tauber. It was the work of Tilman Riemenschneider, was carved towards the end of the 15th century, and depicts a scene from the Last Supper. The figures in the carving are roughly 100 cm high and form the centre panel of a triptych. Riemenschneider came from Heiligenstadt im Eichsfeld in Thuringia, and spent much of his working life in Würzburg, where he had a large workshop employing many craftsmen. He was not just an artist, for he was both imprisoned and tortured as a champion of the rights of the peasants.

The form of lyric poetry known as *Meistergesang* reached its peak in the early 16th century with the work of Hans Sachs of Nuremberg (*left*). Sachs was a shoemaker who composed over 6,000 poems, plays and doggerel verses. (*Opposite, above*) A detail from a wardrobe painting depicting thirteen Meistersänger meeting in Nuremberg. They met together as much to recite as to sing. (*Opposite, below*) The town of Nuremberg, home of the *Meistersänger* Albrecht Dürer and many guilds formed to promote art and poetry.

Although many alchemists still searched for the philosopher's stone that would turn base metals into gold and provide the elixir of life, an ever increasing number sought to apply some of their accumulated wisdom to improve the human condition. (*Above, left*) A modern reconstruction of a medieval alchemist's laboratory, in the Germanisches Nationalmuseum, Nuremberg. (*Below, left*) A medieval country still, from the *Liber de arte distillandi, simplicia et composita* of Hieronymus Brunswig. (*Opposite*) Another illustration from the same work. The apparatus is being used to manufacture aqua vite, a medieval form of brandy.

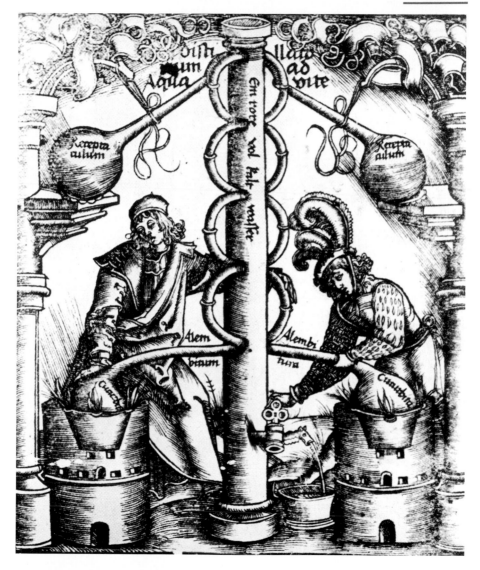

Few people washed regularly. Some argued that water was bad for the body. The Church believed that the sight of one's own nakedness might inspire lewd thoughts. Peasants in general washed neither their bodies nor their clothes. By the 15th century, however, public bath houses were established in most cities and towns of any size. They were places of recreation as much as hygiene, where people met, conversed, listened to music, and had a drink or two. (*Left*) Dürer's engraving of a men's bath.

(*Above*) *Women's Bath* by Hans Sebald Beham, c. 1540. By the mid-16th century, such places had a bad reputation. They were said to be the haunts of prostitutes and adulterers, dens of vice where it was all too easy to contract syphilis (the 'French disease'). Those who worked in such places were denounced. When Albrecht III of Wittelsbach secretly married Agnes Bernauer, the daughter of a bath house proprietor in Augsburg, his father was so infuriated that he arranged to have poor Agnes murdered.

Marriages took place at an early age. It was not uncommon for boys and girls to be betrothed before they reached the age of ten, though the marriage itself might be postponed for two or three more years. (*Above, left*) A priest performs a marriage ceremony in medieval times. On average, a healthy woman could expect to be pregnant between four and eight times in her life. Giving birth (*above, right*) took place at home, and was considered a woman's business. It was extremely rare for a father to attend the birth of his child.

(*Above, left and right*) Two examples of medieval hair styles. '*To dye the hair yellow* – Add enough honey to soften the lees of white wine and keep the hair wet with this all night. Then bruise the roots of celandine and greater olive-madder, mix them with the oil of cumin seed, box shavings and saffron; and keep this on the head for four and twenty hours...' '*To make the hair thick and curly* – Boil maiden hair with smallage seed in wine and oil; or roots of daffydillies, or dwarf-elders, boiled in wine and oil.'

The common round of everyday life was increasingly considered worthy of recording by artists in the 15th century. (*Opposite*) Martin Schongauer's engraving of a peasant family on the way to market, c. 1502. Schongauer was a painter who worked mainly in Colmar. (*Above*) Michael Wolgemut's lively woodcut depicting a scene from his own vivid imagination – *The Dance of Death*.

(*Left*) Albrecht Dürer's copperplate engraving of *The Prodigal Son*, 1500. (*Opposite, above left*) A woodcut of a woman carrying a basket of pies to market. (*Opposite, below left*) A fisherman packing herrings in a barrel. (*Opposite, above right*) A group of surprisingly well dressed agricultural workers, possibly gardeners. (*Opposite, below right*) A woodcut of a 15th-century carpenter, from a design by Michael Wolgemut.

Country people took their pleasures as and when they could find them, but there were certain fixed days for celebration in the calendar. Most villages managed a *fête champêtre*, as recorded by Hans Sebald Beham (*above*). In towns and cities there were often musical recitals (*left*), although most music-making took place at home. (*Opposite, below left*) German musicians perform on the lute, sackbut and harp, from an engraving by Jost Amman. (*Opposite, below right*) An engraving of *Dancers of Christmas Eve*, the impious and wicked who were condemned to dance without stopping for a whole year – a legend of the late 15th century.

For those who could afford it, one of the greatest excitements of medieval life was the hunt. (*Left*) *Die Hirschjagd* by Lucas Cranach, c. 1550. Cranach was born in Kronach, near Bamberg, in 1472 and was court painter at Wittenberg to the Elector Friedrich the Wise of Saxony. (*Above*) A woodcut of a huntsman with falcons, 1491.

Introduction to
Period 2 – 1519–1825

In the 16th century, a new title was given to imperial lands in central Europe: the Holy Roman Empire of the German Nation. It was an advance towards the recognition and construction of a German state, but there was still no distinct German nation on the world map. The components of 'Germany' were there – culture, language, and independence from Rome, especially after the German Reformation of the 1520s. There was even an Imperial Court of Justice (the *Kammergericht*) supported by a permanent Reich tax (the *Gemeine Pfennig*).

Yet still the might of the emperor and the vastness of his empire made it impossible to discern where Germany began and ended. The Emperor Karl V ruled half of Europe – Spain, Sicily, southern Italy, the modern Netherlands and Belgium, Burgundy, Bohemia, Hungary as well as the hereditary Habsburg dominions (*Erblande*). Indeed, many of Karl's problems stemmed from having such a far-flung empire and trying to keep its borders inviolate. In the west he was attacked by France, flexing the new-found muscles of a nation state. In the east he was the bastion of Christian Europe against the hordes of Turkish invaders.

In the rush to follow Columbus across the Atlantic, the Germans were geographically the worst placed of all peoples in Western Europe to share in the spoils of the New World. English, Dutch, French and Portuguese all had a seaboard from which they could launch their expeditions to America. The Germans had none. In the very long run this was to prove at least a relative blessing, for Germany was never tempted to rely on gold or plunder from the rest of the world to finance its economy. The Germans had to develop their own industrial strength, to build and create, to sharpen their talents and hone their skills. No gold-laden galleon was likely to sail into Hamburg harbour in the 16th and 17th centuries.

For much of the period from the beginning of the Reformation to the final defeat of Napoleon Bonaparte in 1815, Germany was the cockpit of Europe. It was the place where battles were fought, where new weapons and tactics jostled each other for military supremacy, where new ideas and ideologies clashed, where new technology was forged in a furnace of rivalry and competition.

The atmosphere of conflict was established by the Reformation itself. In 1517 an obscure monk named Martin Luther wrote a set of ninety-five theses, listing what he saw as abuses within the Catholic Church. Whether he really did nail them to the door of the Castle Church in Wittenberg, we do not know. But the thoughts that the document contained certainly struck at Rome.

Luther did not intend to split the Church. His aim was to purify it, to rid it of these abuses, the worst of which, Luther believed, was the pernicious trade in indulgences. The Church taught that 'good works' or donations of money made during one's lifetime would 'buy' a reduction in the time the soul writhed in Purgatory after death, atoning for one's sins. It was even suggested that this 'time off' could be purchased for someone already dead, for a parent or grandparent, or for any loved one.

Wittenberg was one of many centres for the sale of indulgences and relics – parts of the holy cradle, swaddling clothes of the infant Christ, the remains of innocents slaughtered by Herod. In the year Luther wrote his theses, Johann Tetzel, a papal agent and an accountant to the Fugger bankers, was sent to Wittenberg to raise money by the sale of indulgences. What enraged Luther was the knowledge that the money so raised would be split between Rome and the Fuggers themselves. In Luther's eyes, God, Germany and the poor were all being swindled. In his rage, he sent copies of his theses to the Archbishop of Mainz and the Bishop of Brandenburg.

But the archbishop was deeply in debt to the Fuggers and half his German income came from selling indulgences. He therefore proclaimed Luther a heretic. Three years later Luther was excommunicated, and for the next one hundred and fifty years Germany was torn apart by a succession of wars between Catholics and Protestants. The armies that fought them came from Sweden, Poland, Hungary, Italy and the Habsburg dominions. They marched north, south, east and west, burning farms, villages and towns. They bombarded cities, destroyed crops, killed and looted.

Eventually the wars made way for a new German era: the Age of Absolutism. Despots – benevolent, enlightened or otherwise – established their magnificent courts at Vienna, Dresden, Munich, Mainz and Würzburg. In these courts they fostered the notion of 'courteous conduct' (*Höflichkeit*), and patronised the painters, writers and musicians of the day – Bach and Beethoven, Mozart and Haydn; Gottsched and Schnabel,

Lessing and Goethe. Some of them, notably Friedrich the Great, were artists themselves. Here they also established permanent standing armies. And with the armies came the justification for increased tax collection.

Despite its unpromising situation on the desolate wastes of the 'sand-box of Europe', Brandenburg-Prussia came to be the most powerful component of the new empire. Like the empire itself, Brandenburg-Prussia was a composite, with a large slice of territory (East Prussia) lying outside the borders of the empire. At first the standing army of Prussia was regarded as something of a joke, but after its victories in the many wars of the 18th century it was taken more seriously. The ruling Hohenzollerns were now well-matched rivals of the Habsburgs, and the pattern was set for the next century and a half of German history.

When the fury of the French Revolution of 1789 turned to raw military energy, Germany once again became a battleground. The armies of Russia, France, Austria and Prussia tramped to and fro, fighting on the old fields. From 1794 to 1814 all of Germany west of the Rhine was under French occupation. Attempts were made to delay the end of the Holy Roman Empire by a series of reforms, but these were too few and too late, and the empire was abolished in 1806.

Germany had suffered three hundred years of exhausting conflict and sacrifice, much of it self-inflicted, some of it at the hands of invaders. The Congress of Vienna met under Metternich's wily leadership, to look to the future and search for a new Germany.

7
WARS, MARRIAGES AND THE REFORMATION 1519–1618

(*Right*) *The Planetary Systems*, a woodcut ascribed to Hans
Holbein in the German translation of *The Consolation of
Philosophy* by Boethius. Modern astronomy was founded by
Nicolaus Copernicus, whose mother and father were both
German. At the age of twenty-four, Copernicus was appointed
Canon of Frauenburg, the cathedral city of Ermeland, on the
Frisches Haff. His most famous work was *De Revolutionibus*,
completed in 1530, but not published until 1543, the year of
his death. This brilliant treatise argued that the sun, and not the
earth, was the centre of the universe.

Introduction

Karl V may be reckoned among the greatest of German emperors. He inherited the crown from Maximilian in 1519, a year that was to shake central Europe to its very core. Karl managed to guide his dynasty and his people through the whirlwind whipped up by Luther, with at least the chance of peace after his death in 1553.

The first tremors of the Reformation had scarcely died away before Germany was plunged into the Peasants' War of 1524–5. Peasants and miners took control of Memmingen, Weinburg, Neustadt, Stuttgart and Mülhausen. They were reactionary rather than revolutionary, wanting to put the clock back to what they saw as a better age, a time when peasants had the use of common land and the right to hunt and fish. They were led by the preacher Thomas Müntzer, who was captured, tortured and executed at the age of twenty-eight.

But as well as being an age of furious religious debate and civil war, these were the years of 'prayer, booze and guzzle princes', of a booming German economy, and of revolutionary new thinkers. In the case of Copernicus the ideas were literally revolutionary, for in 1543 he published *De Revolutionibus*, arguing that the sun was the centre of the universe.

Despite the decline of the Hanseatic League, the people of Hamburg maintained their high spirits by drinking a yearly average of 200 gallons of beer per head of population. More soberly, Frankfurt held its first book fair, and Prague became the working home of the astronomers Tycho Brahe and Johannes Kepler.

The century's most eccentric character was Rudolf II, emperor from 1576 to 1612. He was the greatest of the 16th-century private collectors, men and women who believed it was still possible to contain all human knowledge within one's own house. Rudolf's collection of 20,000 objects was housed in four rooms and included stuffed animals, rocks, books, crystals, lenses, plants and a recipe guaranteed to cure the plague. The ingredients were desiccated toad, chicken ovaries, the menstrual blood of a young maiden and white arsenic – all to be baked together and then worn in an amulet next to the heart.

Rudolf declared himself 'Master of Nature', and the curator of his collection described his master's aims: 'The collection should be nothing less than a theatre of the universe...The exhibits act as keys which unlock the whole of human knowledge...The higher purpose is to honour God the Creator.' Visitors to Rudolf's house may well have come away believing that it provided tangible evidence of the existence of Man the Creator.

Martin Luther (*above, left*) was the son of a miner who ran his own copper-smelting business in Mansfeld. Luther intended becoming a lawyer, but was so terrified by a lightning bolt while travelling home one day that he swore by St Anne that he would become a monk. After his initial break with Rome, Luther married Katharina von Bora (*above, right*), a former nun who had withdrawn from convent life. (*Left*) An autograph of Martin Luther, dated 1542.

After being placed under the ban of the Empire by Karl V, Luther took refuge in Wartburg Castle, under the protection of the Elector of Saxony. Here he translated the Bible into German and continued his long-running and acrimonious debate with the Catholic Church. (*Right*) A page from the Lutheran version of the Bible, published in 1534.

On 31 October 1517, Martin Luther published his ninety-five theses on indulgences, possibly by nailing them to the door of Wittenberg Church (*above*). In response, Johann Tetzel burnt Luther's theses and published his own. The tit-for-tat between the rival theologians continued, Luther and a group of radical students burning Tetzel's theses (*left*).

Luther's doctrinal challenge to the teaching of the Church had implications for the temporal authority of the empire. The young Emperor Karl V met with Luther at the Diet of Worms in January 1521 (*above*). Karl hoped that Luther would renounce his heresy. He was disappointed. 'I shall remain true to the words I have written,' announced Luther. 'I do not believe the pope and the councils, for it is obvious that they have often erred and contradicted themselves.'

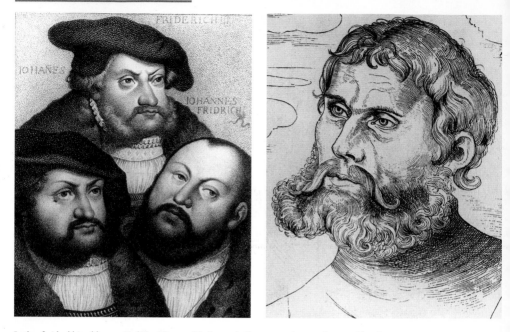

Luther finished his address to Karl V at Worms with the words: 'I cannot act in any other way. Here I stand. God help me. Amen.' It was an uncompromising address, and Luther was well aware of the danger in which he had placed himself. He was excommunicated immediately. Help came from the three 'protectors' of Saxony (*above, left*): Johanes, Friedrich and Johannes Friedrich. Luther travelled in disguise (*above, right*) to the Wartburg in Eisenach (*opposite, above*).

Luther's zeal was undiminished while he sheltered in the castle. He was virtually under house arrest (for his own protection), but continued to preach and expound his forthright views. He spent a year here, writing various treatises and translating the Scriptures, and continually preaching (*right*).

Luther's views spread with extraordinary speed throughout Germany. Among his first converts were many members of the minor clergy and Augustinians, later the backbone of the new Protestant ministry. Much of this was by word of mouth, but the availability of the printed word played a large part. In 1519, only two years after Luther had published his theses in Wittenberg, there were over nine hundred different books printed in Germany, and by 1521 there were more than 500,000 copies of Luther's writings in circulation.

(*Opposite*) An allegorical representation of the Reformation, used to illustrate an early 16th-century book. The 'house' of the Church (though still sheltering Christ) is beset by many reformers, while the pope and his bishops seek to escape by climbing on to the roof. (*Above, left*) Luther is depicted as the Devil's bagpipes in this illustration from Conway's *Demonology,* c. 1540. (*Above, right*) The pope – portrayed as a goat – pipes a different tune in a slightly later illustration.

TOMAS MVNCER PREDIGER ZV ALSTET IN DVRINGEN.

Thomas Müntzer (*left*) was born in Stolberg in the Harz Mountains in 1489. Although claiming to be a follower of Luther, Müntzer's views on Church and society were far more radical. He believed the Apocalypse was about to begin. Denounced by Luther as a fanatic, Müntzer wandered through Germany, preaching to anyone prepared to listen, until elected to be minister of the imperial town of Mühlhausen. Here he sided with rebellious peasants, took up the 'sword of Gideon', and urged the people to make war on the 'fat cats', the princes and the wealthy.

The peasants and the imperial army clashed at Frankenhausen. It was a massacre. Müntzer was captured, tortured until he begged forgiveness and confessed the error of his ways. He was then beheaded on 27 May 1525. His followers were slaughtered in their thousands. Luther wrote: 'The peasants have a bad conscience and an unjust cause...and belong to the devil for all eternity.' (*Far right, above*) German peasants of the early 16th century. (*Right*) A drummer and standard-bearer of the German army at the time of the Peasants' Revolt. (*Below, right*) A group of peasants attack a knight, a woodcut from an edition of Petrarch's *Book of Fortune*, published at Augsburg in 1539.

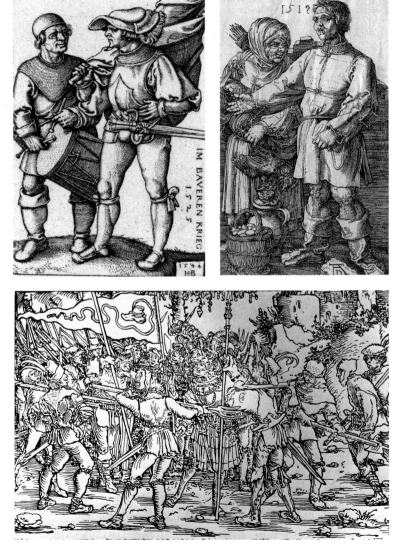

Philip Schwarzerd, known as Melanchthon (*above, left*) was a German Protestant reformer who was born in Breeten in the Palatinate sometime in 1497. He became Professor of Greek at Wittenberg, and an early colleague of Martin Luther. In 1521 he published the *Loci Communes*, reckoned to be the first great Protestant work on dogmatic theology. After Luther's death in 1546, Melanchthon took over the leadership of the German Reformation.

Huldreich Zwingli (*opposite, above right*) was a Swiss reformer who published sixty-seven theses in 1523, outlining his reformed doctrines. Even at this early stage, the Reformation began to fragment into many different movements, each critical of the Catholic Church, but each crucially different from the other. In an attempt to achieve some degree of unity, Zwingli, Luther and others met at Marburg in 1529 (*above*), but the meeting failed to establish any meaningful agreement. Luther and Zwingli clashed over the Eucharist, Zwingli rejecting every form of transubstantiation or consubstantiation.

(*Above*) The Emperor Karl V and Pope Paul III ride out together. Paul III was responsible for the excommunication from the Church of Henry VIII of England in 1538, and for the founding of the Jesuit Order in 1540. His importance in the history of the Holy Roman Empire was that he convened the Council of Trent in 1542, though it did not meet until three years later.

(*Above*) Philip of Hesse pays homage to the emperor after the defeat of the League of Schmalkalden at the Battle of Mühlberg, 24 April 1547. Philip (known as the 'Magnanimous') had established Hesse as a Protestant state, though his regime was tolerant of other faiths. In his thirties he developed syphilis and made a bigamous marriage, which – combined with a lengthy spell of imprisonment after Mühlberg – lessened his influence on European affairs.

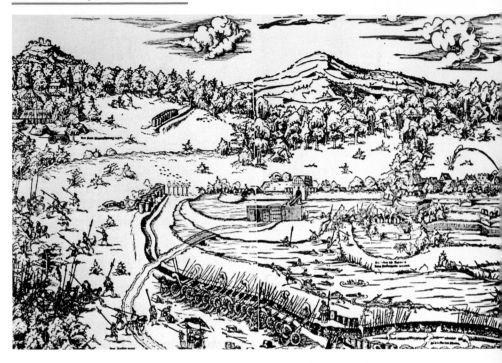

On 27 February 1531, Protestant champions met at Schmalkalden in Thuringia to form a defensive league against the Emperor Karl V. For the next ten years, Karl and his army were heavily occupied in foreign wars, but from 1542 onwards the emperor turned his attention to Germany, for he had sworn to devote 'my kingdoms and powers, my friends, my body, my blood, my life and my soul to the struggle against heresy'. (*Above and right*) Catholics and Protestants clash at the Battle of Wolfenbüttel, January 1542.

Karl V (*opposite and below, left*) was twenty-one when he was crowned emperor at Aachen on 23 October 1520. He spent most of the next thirty years fighting to maintain his empire, protect his religion and extend his overseas dominions. In 1527 he married Isabella of Portugal (*below, right*). They had one son, who became Philip II of Spain. (*Above, right*) The infant Karl is instructed by Erasmus, c. 1510. For most of his childhood, Karl was brought up in Flanders by his aunt, the Archduchess Margaret of Austria.

For most of the 1520s, Karl fought on two fronts. At home he sought to prevent the spread of the 'heresies' of Luther. Abroad he was engaged in a power struggle with Francis I of France for control of northern Italy. In 1525, the imperial armies defeated Francis at the Battle of Pavia (*above*), during which Francis was captured. The French king was later forced to surrender his sword to Karl (*left*).

Although there was a pressing need for him to deal with the Protestant Schmalkaldic League in the early 1530s, Karl's attention was directed eastwards, to Vienna. Suleiman the Magnificent laid siege to the city in 1532 and Karl marched with an army to its relief. After another fierce battle (*above*), the city was saved. (*Right*) A page from a contemporary book offering 'a thorough and faithful account of what recently happened at the siege of Vienna...between those in Vienna and the Turks, from day to day, clearly portrayed, depicted and recounted...'

It was the 'protest' by five evangelical princes and fourteen cities at Speyer in 1529 that gave Protestantism its name. Strongly opposed to such 'heresies' Karl V attended the Diet of Augsburg in 1530 (*above*).

(*Opposite, below right*) Ferdinand I, King of Bohemia and younger brother of Karl V. He was the architect of the compromise at Augsburg in 1555 that brought the religious wars to an end.

(*Opposite, below left*) Part of the settlement of Augsburg placing responsibility for taxation and mustering armies in the control of local estates instead of the emperor.

(*Right*) A code of legal practice which deals with the punishments to be inflicted for a number of offences. Justice was swift and brutal in the 16th century, and the illustration records many favoured methods of punishment – including hanging, imprisonment in the stocks, breaking on the wheel and beheading. There are also several instruments of torture clearly displayed.

Alessandro Farnese was elected pope in 1534, taking the title Paul III (*left*). One of his first acts was to give cardinals' hats to two of his grandsons. Paul was faced with the mounting problem of finding an effective Catholic counter to the Reformation. In 1542 he convoked a General Council of the Catholic Church, though the Council did not meet until 1545 in Trent, and took another eighteen years to reach and publish its conclusions.

(*Above, right*) The inaugural meeting of the Council of Trent in 1542. (*Below, right*) The Council in session. Present were seven cardinals, four arch-bishops, seven prelates, two hundred and twenty-seven bishops, twelve 'heads of religion', twelve doctors of theology, and eight representatives of the principalities. The Council's findings largely reaffirmed the previous teachings of the Catholic Church, rejected Luther's teaching and condemned his translation of the Bible, and stressed the importance of all seven sacraments. Germany was now divided into three religious factions – Catholics, Lutherans and Zwinglians.

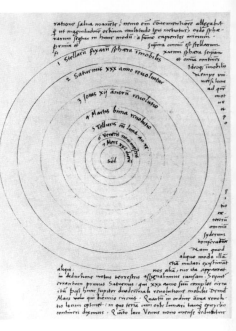

Nicolaus Copernicus (*above, left*) was a man of many talents. As well as being the most brilliant astronomer of his age, he was a bailiff, military governor, judge, tax collector, vicar-general, physician and monetary reformer. His greatest work, however, was to chart the planets and to propose the sun as the centre of the universe. (*Above, right*) A page from the *Copernican Universe* of 1534, showing the position of the planets in relation to the sun.

Like so many new ideas, the development of printing helped to disseminate the findings of Copernicus throughout Germany. He was perhaps fortunate to escape the religious persecution suffered by Galileo a hundred years later. (*Above*) An illustration from a German book of the 16th century showing an old man penetrating the earth's firmament to study the workings of the universe beyond, c. 1550.

ALTERIVS NONSIT QVI SVVS ESSE POTEST

EFIGIES AVREOLI THEOPHRASTI AB HOHEN
HEIM SVE ÆTATIS 47
OMNE DONVM PERFECTVM A DEO
INPERFECTVM A DIABOIO

I SA┼ 40

Rudolf II, Holy Roman Emperor and King of Hungary (*above, left*), was the last of the great medieval collectors and a keen amateur student of medicine. (*Above, right*) Theophrastus Bombastus von Hohenheim, the German alchemist and physician known as Paracelsus. (*Opposite, clockwise from top left*) Four views of 16th-century medical science: an operation for mastoid; a herb garden; a soldier prepares to perform field surgery on a wounded colleague; and a surgeon places a cauterizing iron on a patient's wound.

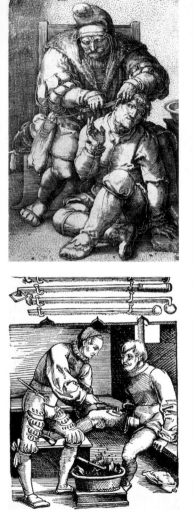

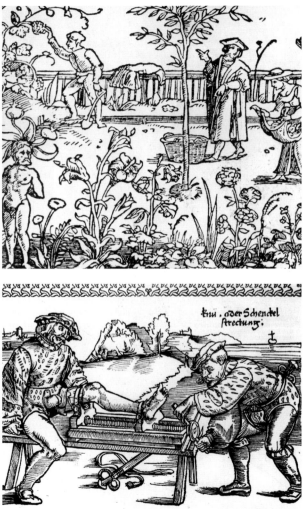

knü. oder Schenckel
ſtreckung:

The German silver industry began in the time of Charlemagne. The absence of gold mines within the empire led to the establishment of a monetary system based on silver coinage. The first silver-bearing lead ore had been found on the hill of Rammelsberg above the town of Goslar in the Harz Mountains, and silver production was well under way in the 11th century. The following century finer silver was discovered near Freiberg. (*Above, left*) The extraction of metal, from the *Cosmographie universelle* of Münster, 1552.

(*Opposite, right*) A German silversmith displays his workmanship in a pair of spurs offered to a customer. (*Right*) The height of craftmanship in silver. A silver elephant made by the German silversmith Christoph Jamnitzer of Nuremberg, some time towards the end of the 16th century. Such works were made as table centrepieces, to enhance the display of wealth and plenty at a feast or banquet. Nuremberg was famous for the intricacy and elaborate design of such work.

Few towns or cities were without their local crafts or industries. Civic pride was often centred around the production of tiles, barrels, carts, glassware, clothing, or any one of a thousand other items. (*Above, left*) A 16th-century smith at work in his foundry, manufacturing cannons and church bells – the skills required were much the same – in this woodcut by Jost Amman. (*Above, right*) Another woodcut by Amman, showing workers in a 16th-century brewery.

VESTIARIVS

(*Above*) The interior of a weaver's workshop – a woodcut by Tobias Stimer, dating from 1558. Although there were cities within the empire (such as Ghent and Bruges) that were famous for weaving and cloth production, the vast majority of material for the ordinary citizen was produced in local workshops such as this. Craftsmen had another two hundred years of such production to look forward to, before the coming of the Industrial Revolution and the factory system swept aside their traditional way of life.

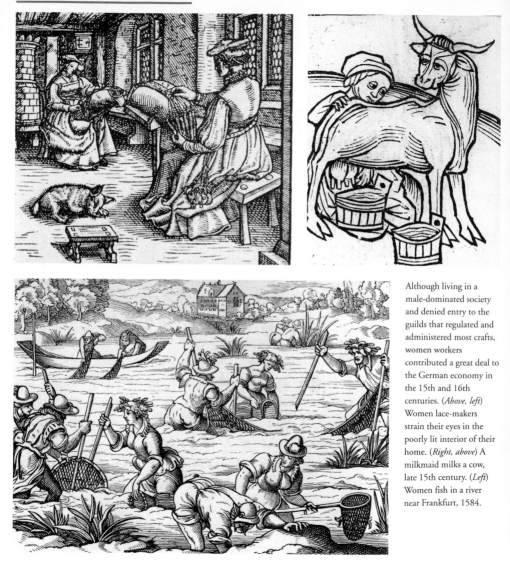

Although living in a male-dominated society and denied entry to the guilds that regulated and administered most crafts, women workers contributed a great deal to the German economy in the 15th and 16th centuries. (*Above, left*) Women lace-makers strain their eyes in the poorly lit interior of their home. (*Right, above*) A milkmaid milks a cow, late 15th century. (*Left*) Women fish in a river near Frankfurt, 1584.

(*Above, right*) A family scene by Johannes Stradanus, c. 1550. Women are engaged in a number of tasks – spinning, sewing and hand-stitching a tapestry – ready at any moment to attend to the child in the playpen, no doubt.
(*Below, right*) A woman milks a ewe, 1549. The milk was almost certainly used to make cheese, and several cheeses are stacked on the shelves in the dairy.

Fashion and style varied enormously from class to class and from one part of Germany to another. Regional costumes were commonly worn, and a seasoned traveller could tell where he or she was simply by studying the clothes of the local population. Female fashion in the 16th century (*clockwise from top left*): a noblewoman of Swabia, 1581; the bridal habit of a lady of Cologne, 1577; the habit of a lady of Silesia, 1577; and the 'ancient habit' of a married woman of Friesland.

Male fashion in the 16th century. (*Above, left*) A wood engraving of a postman by Hans Guldenmund of a postman. The pouch is to hold the letters he carries and the sword is to protect him from thieves. The well-developed calf muscles are to carry him many miles each day. (*Above, right*) A gentleman of Nuremberg, 1577. (*Below, right*) The habit of a senator of Cologne, 1577. (*Below, left*) The habit of a senator from Leipzig in the same year.

Childhood was short-lived in the 15th and 16th centuries. A country boy or girl was expected to share in the labour of his or her parents from a very young age, and even in towns there was little free time to play. (*Above*) A gang of boys bait the city dog warden in 16th-century Strasbourg. (*Left*) A perennial favourite toy – a young boy rides his hobby horse. Note also the toy windmill and the toy falcon that the boy carries on his hand. (*Opposite*) The doll's house of Anna Roferlin, 1631. Anna was clearly a very rich and very lucky little girl.

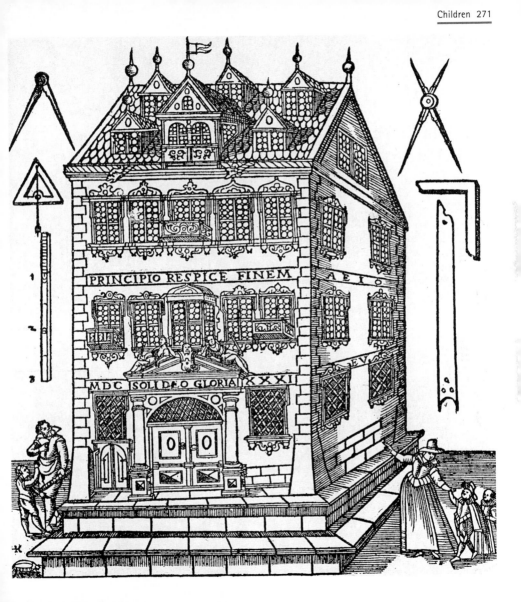

8
THE THIRTY YEARS' WAR 1618–1648

Gustavus Adolphus surveys the battlefield of Breitenfeld, near Leipzig, 17 September 1631. It was one of the decisive battles of the Thirty Years' War, and the first great Protestant victory. Until Breitenfeld, the Catholic armies commanded by Johann Tserclaes Tilly had proved invincible, but in this one battle Tilly lost 20,000 out of his 36,000 men (12,000 killed and 8,000 taken prisoner). Gustavus Adolphus and the Swedes lost only 3,000 men, and Gustavus Adolphus proved his superiority as a general and tactician. But the Thirty Years' War still had another seventeen years to run.

Introduction

The Reformation split the German empire into a patchwork of sectarian strongholds – Catholic, Lutheran, Calvinist and Zwinglian. For much of the first part of the 17th century Germany was embroiled in the Thirty Years' War. In some areas the population was halved. Towns and villages were devastated. Industries collapsed. Land fell into disuse. The slaughter raged until comparative peace was restored at Westphalia in 1648. Twenty years later the writer Hans von Grimmelshausen graphically described the terror and tragedy of these years in his novel *Simplicissimus*, 'the adventures of an unusual vagrant by the name of Melchior Sternfels von Fuchshaim'. It was an immediate success.

Friedrich Wilhelm of Brandenburg-Prussia was greatly affected in his childhood by the law-lessness and suffering of the war, and spent much of his later life seeking to do what he could to rebuild his country. He was also quick to see where his Electorate could profit from the mistakes of others, inviting the Huguenots to Prussia after they had been expelled from France. As a patron of the arts and sciences, he founded the Royal Library, the Art Gallery and the Academy of Science in Berlin. As an astute economist, he promoted the construction of the Friedrich-Wilhelm Kanal, linking the rivers Oder and Spree.

Over much of the empire, government grew stronger. Government bodies became more permanent institutions, rather than assemblies summoned solely at the whim (or desperate need) of the ruling prince. From 1663 the Imperial Diet at Regensburg was a regular congress of ambassadors. Where prince and government worked together the State extended its activities. Greater revenue and newly created or reformed civil services enabled many rulers to subsidise a wide variety of new and old industries. Among those that profited were silk-weavers, tapestry-makers, and soap, tobacco and sugar manufacturers.

With greater prosperity came increased patronage for the arts, and Germany was rich indeed in culture. In 1619 the composer Heinrich Schütz became *Hofkapellmeister* in Dresden, where he introduced styles of music and performance that owed much to Italian influence. German poetry entered a lyric age with the work of Martin Opitz and Andreas Gryphius. Opitz's prose idyll *Daphne* provided the theme for the first truly German opera in 1627. Fifty years later, the first permanent opera house was built in Hamburg. Intellectually, there was much to think about – the works of Leibniz and Spener, the studies on jurisprudence by Freiherr von Pufendorf, the Thomasian lectures, and the contents of the new magazine *Acta Eruditorum*.

But the full flowering of German Baroque was yet to come.

Between May 1608 and June 1609 the empire split into two opposing military leagues – Catholic and Protestant. All that was required for slaughter to begin was a *casus belli*. Events in Bohemia produced it. After Bohemian Protestants built one of their churches on Catholic land, the leaders of their community were thrown into gaol and the church was demolished. In revenge, Protestant notables broke into Hradschin Castle on 23 May 1618, and threw two Catholic officials out of a window (*opposite, below*). The officials were unharmed, landing safely on a dung heap 45 feet below. The Catholics now found a new leader in the Emperor Ferdinand II (*above, left*) whose wife was Eleanora Gonzaga (*above, right*).

Ferdinand's imperial army proved too much for the young Bohemian king, Friedrich V, elector of the Palatinate, whose troops were annihilated at the Battle of the White Mountain near Prague on 8 November 1620. (*Right*) Friedrich V with his wife Elizabeth – the 'Winter Queen' and daughter of Charles I of England. After the Battle of the White Mountain the two became political refugees, wandering unhappily through Europe.

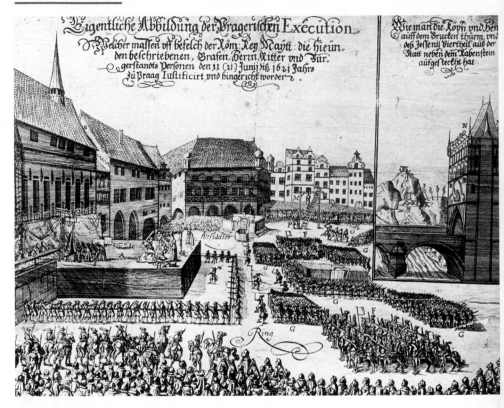

Bohemia paid a high price for its unsuccessful rebellion against the authority of the emperor. Prague was occupied by the Catholic army and many of its nobles and citizens were publicly executed (*above*). Those who dared to shelter or aid the former rebels were hunted down and in many cases murdered in their own houses (*opposite*).

The initial victories of the Catholic armies brought mercenaries flocking to support the emperor (and hunt for booty). The greatest of them was Albrecht von Wallenstein (*opposite*), a cavalry officer of considerable skill. Others, however, signed up to back the Protestant cause. In December 1625 England, Denmark, the United Provinces and Friedrich V signed an alliance at The Hague, and the Danes under Christian IV (*right*) invaded Germany. They were defeated by Wallenstein and Tilly at Lutter am Barenberg. (*Above*) Philips Wouwerman's painting of a cavalry skirmish during the Thirty Years' War.

Both sides committed appalling atrocities. In May 1630 General Tilly (*above*) captured the city of Magdeburg after a lengthy siege. In what he called the 'Magdeburg Wedding', Tilly allowed his troops to indulge in an orgy of murder, rape and pillage, at the end of which the city was completely destroyed (*left*). The long-term effect of this was to harden the Protestant resolve to fight on.

Tilly was killed two years later, and the tide of battle began to flow in the Protestants' favour. At the Battle of Lützen (*right*), Gustavus Adolphus (*top*) defeated Wallenstein, but was himself mortally wounded. (*Above*) Irish mercenary troops in the service of Gustavus Adolphus at the time of the Battle of Lützen.

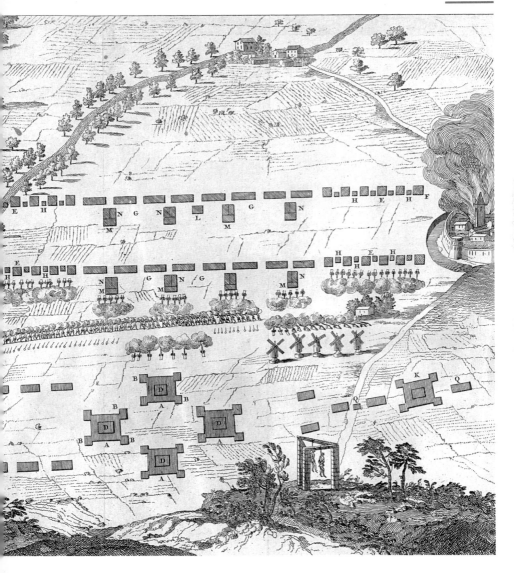

The carnage continued. The Swedish statesman Axel Oxenstierna (*above, right*) united the German Protestants in the League of Heilbronn. Karl Gustav Wrangel, who replaced Gustavus Adolphus as commander of the Swedish army, was defeated by Ferdinand of Hungary at the Battle of Nördlingen (*above, left*) in November 1634. (*Opposite, below*) Wrangel is surprised and almost captured by imperial troops during a hunting expedition.

Eigentlicher Abriß wie das GENERAL Friedlandt von dem Obristen Leüttnampt Gordan zu Eger ist erstochen worden Anno 1634.

Wallenstein's skills as a general were not backed by political wisdom. He plotted behind the emperor's back, making overtures to Saxony, France and even Sweden. On 25 February 1634 he was assassinated by Scots and Irish officers of his staff in Eger Castle, Bohemia. (*Left*) Wallenstein is depicted as a maverick, prepared to ride any mount to get what he wants. (*Above*) Four scenes from the assassination of Wallenstein, showing his murder and the disposal of his body.

In 1637 Ferdinand, King of Hungary and Bohemia (*Above, right*), was elected Emperor Ferdinand III. He had conspired in the overthrow and murder of Wallenstein, and personally succeeded him as commander of the imperial armies. For the rest of the war he was in charge of Catholic and imperial fortunes in Germany. (*Below, right*) A graphic portrayal of the 'total war' waged by Catholics and Protestants alike between 1618 and 1648. Prisoners-of-war were often killed. Innocent peasants were massacred. Entire communities were destroyed.

Eventually the killing stopped, with both sides exhausted and fearful that the empire was now too weak to defend itself against foreign predators. Representatives from both sides met in the town hall of Münster in May 1648 to negotiate the treaty that became known as the Peace of Westphalia (*above*). Sweden made extensive gains in western Pomerania. The Protestants held on to the land they occupied in 1624. The Catholics were the main losers. (*Opposite*) A messenger rides through Germany, bringing the joyous news of peace from Münster, 1648.

Neuer
Auß Münster vom 25. deß Weinmonats im Jahr
1648. abgefertigter Freud- vnd Friedenbringender Postreuter.

Ich komm von Münster her gleich Spor:nstreich ge-
ritten/
Vnd habe nun das meist deß Weges überschritten/
Ich bringe gute Post vnd neue Friedenszeit/
der Frieden ist gemacht/ gewendet alles Leid.
Man läßt ihn freudig auß mit hellen Feldtrommeten/
mit Kesselpauck Hall/ mit klaren Feld-Clareten.
Mercur fliegt in der Lufft/ vnd auch der Friede; Jot
Gantz Münster/Oßnabrugg vnd alle Welt ist froh/
die Glocken thönen starck/ die Orgeln lieblich klingen/
Ihr Herr Gott wil loben dich/ für Freud die Leute singen/
die Stücke donneren vnd saußen in der Lufft/
die Fahnen steigen schön/vnd als jauchzend rufft:
der Höchste sey gelobt/der Friede ist getroffen/
fortan ein männiglich ein besser Jahr zu hoffen/
der Bauer und der Pflug/ der Ochse und das Pferd.

Die Kirchen werden fort in voller Blüh stehen/
Man wird zum Hauß deß HErren in vollen Sprüngen gehen/
und hören Gottes Wort: Kunst wird seyn hochgeacht/
die Jugend wird studirn bey Tag und auch bey Nacht/
Man wird der HErren Ruhen auff Plätzen und auff Seilen/
In Osten und in Westen/ in Nord außbreiten :
die Saline und Paris/die Donau und die Wien/
der Friede und sein Stockholm sind friedlich frisch und grün.

Der Friede kömt Gott lob mit schnellem Flug geflogen/
mit ihm kompt alles Glück und Segen eingezogen/
Er bringet Friedensfloß und güldene Friedens-Zeit/
der Krieg ist nun ausstirbt/ gerufet alles Leid.
Sieg/ Segen/ Schild und Schwerdt/ und Lantzen sind zerschmissen/
Gerechtigkeit und Fried sich miteinander küssen/
Wo Mars der Landesherr Gott/die Oberherrschafft hat
da herrschet Lasterschwarm/ und Tugend hat nicht statt.
Drum freuet/freuet Euch ihr hohen Potentaten/
und alle die ihr müßt den grossen Städten rathen/

Fortan wird Land und Sand und Dörffer nehmen zu/
und Herr und Knecht wird sein in angenehmer Ruh.
Es werden Fürsten nicht in Cantzeleien schwitzen/
der Naht nicht in die Nacht mit schweren Sorgen sitzen/
und dencken/wo doch Rath wol herzunehmen sey/
damit betreuer werd deß Krieges Tyranney.
Man wird Städte seyn bedacht/wie rechte Sach mög bleiben/
Wie man nun unrecht ist/recht mäge hindertreiben/
Man wird nicht so versehn was böses wird verricht/
wie sonst zu Kriegszeit/doch eyne Lust geschicht/
Es werden Obrigkeit und Unterthanen wohnen
in Einigkeit und Fried : das gute wird man lohnen/
das böß straffen ab Kurtz : es wird Friede seyn/
im Rathhauß/in der Stadt/wo man gehet auß und ein.
Ihr Obern dancket Gott/der Friede ist gericht/
Ihr Untern lobet Ihn/ das wild jaist geschlichtet/
Es lest im Feld und Freud der Nahebern und die Stadt/
Ist das was in der Welt und Sie im Ruhe hat.

Auch Id der Kauffleute Herr Mercur koht hergedrungen/
und hab mich mit dem Brieff durch Lufft und Lufft geschwungen/
Ihr Kauffleut frot wolauff und habt ein guten Math/
Ihr Handwercks Leute auch/es wird alle werden gut.
Fort wird man sicherlich zu Wasser können handeln/
und ohne Gefahr zu Land auff Messen ruhig wandeln/
die Waaren werden und zu reissen abgesetzt/
die Läden und Gewölb wol lauter Kauffer stehn/
Man wird zu Tag für Tag den Seidenzeug auffmessen/
und zu Mittag für Näht nicht einen bissen essen/
Gewürtz und Specerey verlauffen wol ein Macht/
bey lauter Centnern wegen/gen Tag und Nacht.
Der Schuster wird sein Geld vor Schuh nicht können zehlen/
Der Schneider wird das Volck und neue Kleider quelen/
Der Breuer nimbt nicht ab/der Becker der wird reich/
Der Kürschner sattet seiden/und freuet keinen Streich/
Es leben bey dem Feur die Schmid/die Ambosschläger/
Es tantzen mich allein die armen Degenfeger/

Die haben nichts zu thun : Laßt Degen/Degen seyn/
machet eine Pflug darfür/und eine Pflugschaar drein.

Ihr Bauren spannet an die starcken Ackerpferde/
fliaschet mit der Peitschen scharff/die Pflugschaar in die Erde/
Säet/Hirschet/Heidel/Korn/Hanff/Weitzen auß/
Kraut/Ruben/Zwiebeln/Kohl/füll Keller/Boden/Hauß.

Ihr Gärtner werdet dann zu Marckt können fahren/
und lösen manchen Batz auß euren grünen Waaren/
dann lehret mit Lust ein in ein Küchlein ein/
und legt ein stärklein Wurst wol lesch den Durst mit Wein/
Juch/ Juch/ihr seyd befreyt von tausend tausend Plösen/
und schaffet biß zu tags mit euren Bauren Dreesen.

Ihr Wirthe freut euch auch/der Friede trägt euch ein/
Es wird die Stub und Stall voll Gast und Pferde seyn/
Voran die ihr wol ligt/beym weiß rotten Hanen/
Beim Baum/beym Engel/Stern/Wolff/Lamm/Löwen/Thurnen/Schwan/
Beim Bieterhold/beim Creutz/Glaß/Nußfaß/Rädlein/Tisch/
beim wilden Mann/Kron/Mond/beim güldnen Ochsen/Fisch/
Beim Ochsenfelder/wol/Ihr krieget gute Zechen/
Ihr wolt denn selbsten nicht/die Zech Wirthisch machen/
doch glaub ich gäntzlich nicht : Nun es ben keine Noth/
Ein jeder gebe mir ein gutes Botenbrodt.

Doch dieses alles recht mit beten und mit dancken/
daß keiner überschreit der Erbarkeiten Schrancken/
Es dancke alles Gott/es dancke Ihm frü vnd spat/
was kreucht/seugt/lebt und schwebt/ und was nur
Othem hat.

One of the few German territories to emerge enlarged and strengthened from the war was the electorate of Brandenburg, under the control of Friedrich Wilhelm, the Great Elector (*above, left*). Although the newly created Brandenburg-Prussia was too poor to generate the capital for modernisation, Friedrich Wilhelm's skilful diplomacy enabled him to wrest control of taxation from the imperial courts. The component states of the empire were steadily increasing their independence. (*Above, right*) Louise Henriette of Orange, wife of the Great Elector. (*Opposite*) The equestrian statue of the Great Elector by Andreas Schlüter in Berlin.

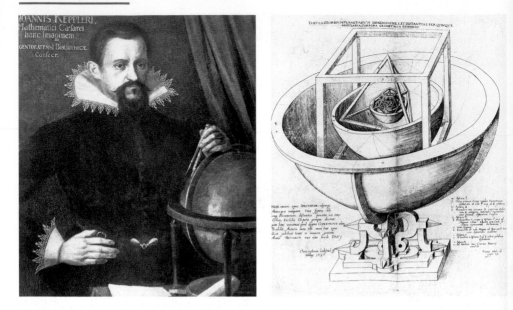

While the war raged across Germany, there were still those who managed to create rather than destroy, to advance knowledge rather than resort to barbarity. Johannes Kepler (*above, left*) was one of the greatest scientists of the late 16th and early 17th centuries. He was the astronomer who discovered the motion of the planets round the sun. (*Above, right*) A late 16th-century diagram of Kepler's model to show how the planets moved. (*Opposite, below*) The divine musical scales of each planet, from Kepler's *Harmonies Mundi* of 1619. (*Opposite, above*) A 17th-century German observatory.

Saturnus Jupiter Mars ferè Terra

Venus Mercurius Hic locum habet etiam

One of the many scientists for whom the Great Elector acted as patron was Otto von Guericke of Magdeburg (*left*). Guericke conducted experiments on the properties of a vacuum, sealing two hemispheres together, and then extracting the air from within with a modified water pump. To prove the strength of the vacuum thus created, Guericke harnessed a team of horses to each hemisphere, pulling in opposite directions in an attempt to pull the spheres apart (*above*).

To Guericke's satisfaction and to the amazement of many onlookers, including the emperor at Regensburg (where the experiment was conducted), this proved impossible. Guericke was a student of law, mathematics, fortifications and, crucially, mechanics, who had acted as an engineer to the Swedish army in the Thirty Years' War. (*Right*) Two further experiments into the properties of what Guericke called the 'Magdeburg Spheres'.

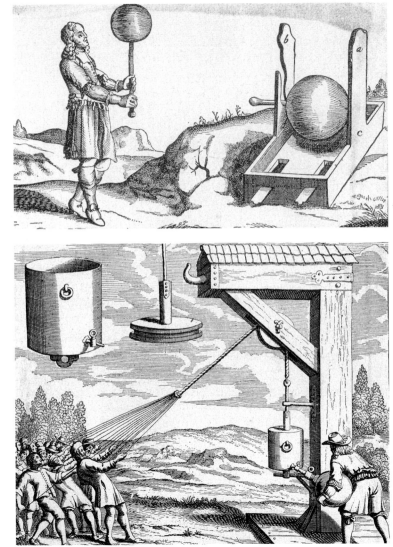

Hall in Sachsen
Gegen Abend

(*Opposite, left*) Martin Opitz, a leading German poet of the early 17th century. (*Opposite, below right*) Gottfried Wilhelm Leibniz, the great German mathematician, philosopher and historian. (*Opposite, above right*) The title page of Hans Jakob Christoffel von Grimmelshausen's novel *Simplicissimus*, set in the Thirty Years' War. (*Right*) The composer Heinrich Schütz. (*Far right*) The painter Matthäus Merian, and (*above*) Merian's engraving of Halle.

As the threat of war drifted away, the full glories of early baroque art and architecture were revealed throughout Germany. (*Above*) The castle and Dom dominate the skyline of Salzburg in Austria, one of the most beautiful cities in 17th-century Europe. (*Opposite*) The grand staircase of the residence of the Prince-Bishop of Würzburg, designed by Balthasar Neumann, with paintings added later by Tiepolo. Neumann was perhaps the greatest master of the early years of German Baroque.

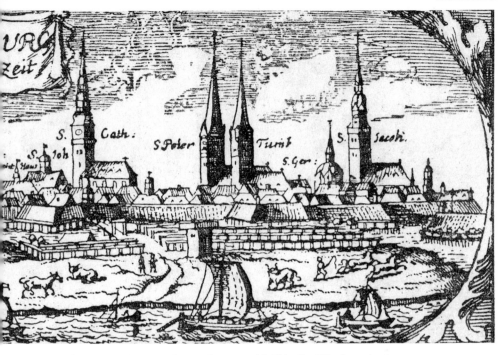

Some cities were fortunate enough to escape the worst destruction of the Thirty Years' War. One such was Hamburg, which remained economically strong throughout the 17th century. (*Above*) An engraving of Hamburg in 1696, on the confluence of the rivers Elbe and Alster. (*Opposite*) An illustration of a busy German port which accompanied a set of printed rules for the behaviour of merchants in the second half of the 17th century, entitled 'Well meaning reminders for the young merchant and tradesman by which he should regulate himself if he does not wish to be ruined…' – an early self-help book.

When peace returned to Germany in 1648, most states were in a desperate plight. Agriculture had been badly hit, with much previously cultivated land returning to the wild. Despite woefully poor harvests, the price of corn fell dramatically, adding widespread poverty to undernourishment. Some of the old independent cities and principalities were simply too small to survive economically. Elsewhere recovery was slow, but was gradually realised thanks to the injection of new capital. Friedrich Wilhelm and others encouraged a variety of industries, including silk weaving, tapestries, soap, sugar and tobacco.

Money makes the world go round... (*Opposite*) A mid-17th-century picture of the good side of borrowing. The availability of money stimulates trade, leading to profit for all. Such illustrations served to kick-start the German economy in the years immediately following the Peace of Westphalia. (*Above*) Workers in a German mint in the 17th century. Coins were still hand-minted by hammering a die on to a disc of metal – usually silver. The man in the centre is weighing the newly struck coins to make sure each contains the required amount of metal. In the yard outside the metal is smelted.

Tobacco reached Germany from the New World in the 16th century. (*Left*) One of the hundreds of smoking-clubs established in towns and villages throughout the empire. (*Above*) Three early 17th-century celebrations of the joys of smoking.

9
WAR AND PEACE
1698–1790

The choir and dome of the pilgrims' church of the Scourged
Saviour, Steingaden – known as the Wieskirche – built by
Dominikus Zimmermann in the 1740s, and the finest achievement of the Wessobrunn school. The dazzling blue and gold of
the decoration almost masks the architectural structure of the
building itself. It is difficult to see where essential pillars and
supports end and sumptuous Baroque ornamentation begins.
The church owes its existence to a farmer's wife, who found a
statue of a weeping Christ discarded by monks. So many pilgrims
flocked to the simple shrine made by her husband that Zimmermann was commissioned to build a church to house the statue.

Introduction

German art and architecture reached their most decorative Baroque glory. Castles, houses, churches, palaces, hunting-lodges and town halls glittered and glowed with golden embellishment, and dripped with ornate detail like wedding cakes carved from marble. The number of these ripe masterpieces reflects a new-found opulence: Sanssouci at Potsdam; the Schloss Charlottenburg, Berlin; the Zwinger at Dresden; the Residenz, Würzburg; the pilgrimage church of Vierzehnheiligen; the Weissenstein Palace, Pommersfelden, and many more.

The rich who sauntered through these marbled halls were dressed *à la mode*, for costume, cooking, manners, deportment, everything had to follow the dictates of Paris. Everything except the music – which was undeniably and magnificently German. In Bach, Telemann, Haydn and Mozart, Germany produced a quartet of genius never to be equalled. At Mannheim, the violin virtuoso Johann Stamitz established the sound of the modern orchestra. In Prussia Friedrich II wrote his sonatas and played his flute, corresponded with Voltaire, grabbed Upper and Lower Silesia and a large slice of Poland, and generally made his country powerful and prosperous.

Women married younger and produced more children, though smallpox, typhus and tuberculosis were rampant and on average only 50 per cent survived. A quarter of Germany's population still lived in poverty, but there was work to be found in the new factories that were replacing the old artisan workshops.

Great minds turned away from the traditional professions. Schiller struggled through unhappy experiences as an army doctor, and then found fulfilment in the *Sturm und Drang* of his verse and plays. Goethe abandoned the law and set off on a similar literary career. Gotthold Ephraim Lessing started adult life as a theology student, but also turned to writing. Immanuel Kant had no such false starts, producing his great works of philosophy towards the end of the 18th century: *Kritik der reinen Vernunft* (1781), *Kritik der praktischen Vernunft* (1788) and *Kritik der Urteilskraft* (1790). The more prolific Johann Jakob Moser began publication of his fifty-one-volume treatise on German law in 1757.

There was an explosion in the number of newspapers, magazines, broadsheets, pamphlets and journals of all sorts. Scientific and political societies identified and defined a German nation long before princes and statesmen were able to. Johann Gottfried von Herder was the spearhead of the cultural nationalism movement, championing the notion of a cultural community – a *Volk*. And when Friedrich II introduced the unpopular salt tax, and people turned to vinegar as an alternative preservative, he inadvertently prompted one of the 18th century's longest surviving creations – the gherkin.

Friedrich II (*opposite*) – 'the Great' – was brought up under a rigid system of education and strict military discipline. (*Below, right*) The young Friedrich with his sister Wilhelmina. At the age of eighteen Friedrich made a vain attempt to run away to England and would have been executed by his father but for the intervention of the Emperor Karl VI. He later became a popular monarch, mixing freely with his people (*above, right*), though often plagued by debt. (*Below, left*) A letter from Friedrich acknowledging a debt of 32,000 Reichsthalers to the burghers of Potsdam.

Friedrich II earned the nickname 'the Great' from the part he played in a series of Silesian Wars against Austria. In the 1740s he took up arms against the Empress Maria Theresia (*above, left*), reviving an ancient claim to Silesia. In 1759 Friedrich defeated the Austrians at the Battle of Kunersdorf (*opposite, above*). (*Opposite, below*) Friedrich and his staff review his troops. Jealousy of Austrian power led Friedrich to take part in the partition of Poland in 1772, by which Brandenburg-Prussia gained Polish Prussia and a portion of Greater Poland. (*Above, right*) *The Cake of Kings*, a contemporary depiction of the partition.

Like many rulers in the late 18th century, Friedrich the Great was a man of culture and accomplishment. He was particularly fond of music, and was a composer and flautist of considerable ability. (*Above*) Friedrich plays the flute at *The Concert at Sanssouci* by Adolf von Menzel. (*Below, left*) Georg Philipp Telemann, the most prolific composer of the early 18th century. Telemann wrote forty-four passions, forty operas, countless songs and oratorios and a large amount of orchestral music. (*Opposite*) The music-room at the Palace of Sanssouci.

(*Opposite*) The exterior of Georg Wenzeslaus von Knobelsdorff's magnificent Marble Hall in the Palace of Sanssouci, built for Friedrich the Great in the late 1740s. (*Left*) The interior of the entrance hall at Sanssouci, begun in 1745. (*Below, left*) A detail of the ornamental pavilion and (*below, right*) a detail from an ornate ceiling, both at Sanssouci.

Among the many frequent and brilliant visitors to Friedrich's palace at Sanssouci was the French writer and philosopher François-Marie Arouet de Voltaire (*left*). The two discussed the topics of the age, and Voltaire occasionally read aloud from his works to Friedrich (*above*). (*Below*) The signature of Friedrich the Great. (*Opposite*) *The Round Table at Sanssouci* from the painting by Adolf von Menzel. Other illustrious guests included Maupertuis, Francesco Algarotti and Jean Baptiste d'Argens.

In the 1680s Matthias Daniel Pöppelmann was one of a trio of distinguished architects who arrived in Dresden. By the end of the 17th century, Friedrich August, Elector of Saxony (*opposite far right, centre*), had commissioned Pöppelmann to build the astoundingly beautiful Zwinger, near Dresden (*right*). (*Opposite far right, above*) Moritzburg Castle, a later creation of Pöppelmann. (*Opposite far right, below*) Early examples of Meissen ware, fine porcelain china from the 17th-century factory on the outskirts of Dresden.

The Sultan Mustapha II of Turkey (*far left*) spent most his short reign fighting the Austrians. On 11 September 1697, at the Battle of Zente (*above and opposite*), his Turkish army was defeated by Austrian and imperial troops under the command of Prince Eugen of Savoy (*left*). Two years later, Mustapha II was forced by the Treaty of Karlowitz to cede much of the territory he held in the Balkans. He spent the rest of his reign attempting to stifle revolts within his own empire.

Die St. THOMAS Kirch in LEIPZIG mit anligenden Gebæuen.

The greatest composer of the 18th century (and possibly of all time) was Johann Sebastian Bach (*far left*). Bach mixed inspiration with perspiration – composing, teaching, playing, and fathering thirteen children. (*Above*) The Church of St Thomas, Leipzig, where Bach was choirmaster for twenty-seven years.

(*Right*) Another musical giant from Germany in the 18th century – Georg Friederich Händel. He was born in Halle in 1685 and became organist of Halle Cathedral at the age of seventeen. He was also a violinist and conductor, but is best remembered for his operas (*Rinaldo, Alcina*), oratorios (*The Messiah*) and orchestral music (*Water Music, Music for the Royal Fireworks, Saul, Israel in Egypt*, etc). (*Opposite, below right*) The manuscript of the first page of J. S. Bach's *Well-Tempered Clavier*, c. 1730, one of many masterpieces he wrote for various keyboard instruments.

If J. S. Bach has a serious rival for the title 'greatest composer of all time', that rival must be Wolfgang Amadeus Mozart – (*top, left*) at the age of seven in 1763, and (*opposite, below right*) as a young man. Mozart was a child prodigy. He played the piano confidently at the age of four and composed his first piano pieces a year later. By the time he was eleven, Mozart was accompanying his father Leopold and his sister Marianne at public recitals (*top, right*). (*Above*) Mozart's autograph.

Mozart's brilliant forerunner and later contemporary was Franz Joseph Haydn (*right*), who revolutionised the form and content of both the orchestral symphony and the string quartet. Haydn quickly recognised the genius of Mozart, but was less certain of the talent of Beethoven, one of his own pupils. (*Above*) A page from Haydn's manuscript arrangement of his own Austrian national anthem for a string quartet.

The rich musical wealth of Germany was matched in literature. Johann Wolfgang von Goethe (*left*) was a poet, dramatist, scientist and court official from Frankfurt. He was also an enthusiastic watercolour artist, as an illustration from his *Italienische Reise* (*below*) shows, and a dabbler in alchemy, anatomy and antiquities.

In his Frankfurt study (*above, right*), he wrote some of his many dramas, including *Götz von Berlichingen*, *Faust* and *Hermann und Dorothea*. *Faust* was his masterpiece and the labour of his life, for it took him many years to complete. More than two hundred years after he wrote it, the play is considered one of the classics of world literature. (*Above, left*) An anatomical drawing from Goethe's *Italienische Reise*, dating from the 1790s.

Goethe's literary twin peak was Johann Christoph Friedrich von Schiller, born at Marbach on the Neckar in 1759. Schiller was a historian, dramatist and (most notably) a poet, though his intended profession was medicine. As a young man Schiller began writing his *Sturm und Drang* poetry and plays, works that were passionate and revolutionary. His most famous play is perhaps *Don Carlos*, written in blank verse and completed in 1787. (*Left*) A bust of Schiller by the German sculptor Dannecker.

Schiller's greatest poems come from the 1790s. His greatest plays – *Die Jungfrau von Orleans*, *Maria Stuart*, *Die Braut von Messina* and *Wilhelm Tell* – were written slightly later. (*Above*) Schiller gives a private performance of part of *Don Carlos* at the court of the Grand Duke Karl August of Weimar, 1788. The melodramatic style of acting and delivery of the time was well suited to the intensity of Schiller's writing. (*Right*) Part of a letter written by Schiller towards the end of his life.

Goethe and Schiller were not the only German writers who flourished in the late 18th century. Christoph Martin Wieland (*above, left*) produced the first German translation of Shakespeare, and wrote much elegant, fashionable and graceful poetry. (*Above, right*) Friedrich Gottlieb Klopstock, another German poet. (*Left*) A 'league' of young poets from the University of Göttingen in the 1770s. (*Opposite*) A lively illustration from Rudolf Erich Raspe's *Baron Münchausen's Narrative of His Marvellous Travels and Campaigns in Russia*.

The greatest German philosopher of the 18th century was Immanuel Kant (*left*), Professor of Logic and Metaphysics at Königsberg University in East Prussia, whose controversial views on religion caused Friedrich Wilhelm II to ban him from writing on religious subjects. Johann Christoph Gottsched (*opposite, below left*) was Professor of Poetry and Philosophy at Leipzig (*opposite, above*). Christian von Wolff (*opposite, below right*) was a philosopher, mathematician and scientist, and a pupil of Leibniz.

(*Left*) The interior of the
Church of the Virgin,
Birnau, designed by the
sculptor and stuccoist
Joseph Anton Feuchtmayr
and built between 1748
and 1750. Such extensive
detail and ornament has
never been surpassed in a
church interior. (*Opposite*)
The interior of the
Benedictine Church
of Zwiefalten in
Baden-Württemberg,
designed by Johann
Michael Fischer and built
between 1738 and 1765.
The eye is drawn by the
long nave, past the grey
and rose marble columns,
the gold leaf, the white
walls, the paintings and
the balustrades, and is
then lifted up to the
paintings on the ceilings.

In the late 1720s and 1730s, the Elector Clement Augustus commissioned the building of a hunting-lodge of palatial proportions at Brühl. The initial builder of what became known as the Augustusburg (*opposite, above*) was Johann Conrad Schlaun, though he was later replaced by the Munich court architect, François de Cuvilliès. (*Left*) The staircase hall of the Augustusburg, designed by Balthasar Neumann and constructed between 1741 and 1744. The paintings were the work of Carlo Carlone.

Clement Augustus died before the Augustusburg was finally completed, though he did live long enough to see some of the sumptuous decoration of the interior. Much of the work here was also to the designs of Carlo Carlone, in particular the Nepomuk Chapel (*right*) and the glorious dining-room (*far right*). He received 5,325 imperial thalers for his work.

Among the many glories of German High Baroque were the carvings and sculptures that decorated church and cathedral, palace and memorial. German artists worked in wood, stone, bronze and plaster to produce a body of work that was among the finest and the richest in the world. (*Left*) Matthias Rauchmiller's marble carving for the tomb of Karl von Metternich in the Frauenkirche, Trier. The informal quality of the figure was a break with tradition, suggesting a moment in the life of the man rather than an attempt to overawe the viewer.

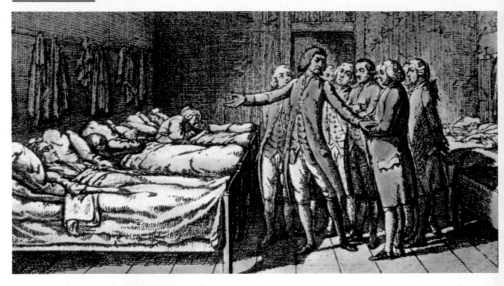

Science had charted the movement of the planets, identified the laws of gravity, revolutionised warfare – but had been unable to do much in the way of combating disease and illness. Christian Friedrich Samuel Hahnemann (*left*) was a physician and the founder of homeopathy. He was born at Meissen in 1755 and studied medicine at Leipzig. After many experiments on the curative powers of bark, he decided that medicines produced in healthy people similar symptoms to those it attempted to cure in the sick. He therefore prescribed infinitesimal doses of medicine, incurred the wrath of the apothecaries and was driven out of every town in which he tried to practise from 1798 to 1810.

Two contemporary illustrations of mainstream medical practice in the 18th century. (*Opposite, above*)
The sickroom of a hospital in 1782, from a drawing by Chodowiecki. (*Above*) The Pesthof in Hamburg,
1746. The plague was still an almost annual visitor to most German towns and cities, especially to those
old centres of population where people lived in cramped and close proximity to each other. In the illustration the windows appear to be tightly closed, evidence that it was still commonly believed that one of
the causes of the plague was 'bad air'.

Daniel Chodowiecki was a Polish artist who toured much of Europe making sketches of the everyday working life of tradesmen and artisans. Many of his illustrations were used in the early 18th-century encyclopaedia published by Basedon. (*Above, left*) Chodowiecki's drawing of the interior of a German coachbuilder's. (*Below, left*) Spinning, knitting and lace-making in the 18th century. Most women were expected to be mistresses of more than one such craft.

Two more illustrations by Chodowiecki. (*Above, right*) Men employed in a metal workshop. It appears that they are probably making wire, and that the machine in the foreground is being used to stretch the length of metal. (*Below, right*) A detailed drawing of the interior of a cabinet-maker's. Some men are preparing wood, others are fitting panels to cupboards or dressers. In the foreground a man is boiling up glue. Some of the tools being used have changed little in the last two hundred and fifty years.

10
REVOLUTION AND FEDERATION
1790–1825

(*Right*) Napoleon Bonaparte rides in triumph through the centre of Dusseldorf, 3 November 1811. The city that had been the capital of the Palatinate had been invaded by French landscape gardeners and designers throughout the latter half of the 18th century, but this invasion was considerably more exciting. Bonaparte had expected Germany to be grateful for the introduction of French ideas and the French legal system. He was mistaken. Although reforms were achieved, many German states saw Bonaparte as little better than a pirate, plundering his former enemies to support his own regime.

Introduction

The ever-growing rivalry between Prussia and Austria was halted by events in France. In 1791 both nations agreed to act together to save Louis XVI and the French royal family from the worst excesses of the French Revolution. The outcome was a series of catastrophic defeats for the Prussian army – at Valmy (1792), Austerlitz (1805) and Jena (1806) – and the abolition of the Holy Roman Empire.

Something had to be done to restore Prussian, if not all German, military pride. The Prussian Order of the Iron Cross was inaugurated during the Napoleonic Wars, at a time when the continental blockade imposed by Bonaparte prevented the import of British steel, thereby also leading to an increase in the production of German iron costume jewellery. In 1810 Scharnhorst founded the War Academy and introduced the short-service system of recruitment that was later to be adopted by all armies. Blücher restored morale with the defeat of Napoleon at Waterloo, and Carl von Clausewitz became Director of the General War School in Berlin. Later his textbook *Vom Kriege* (*On War*) became the bible for all military strategists.

Other major reforms of a more constructive nature were to be seen in German education. As Minister of Education Wilhelm Freiherr von Humboldt founded the Friedrich Wilhelm University in Berlin, and supervised the establishment of new elementary and secondary schools, including the elite grammar schools (*Gymnasia*).

The philosopher Georg Wilhelm Friedrich Hegel set out his famous dialectic in his *Wissenschaft der Logik* (*Science of Logic*) in 1816, sending progressive intellects racing down a road that led to Marxism, Existentialism and Positivism. No doubt guests at Rahel Varnhagen

von Ense's salon wrestled with these complicated new ideas. The students of Wartburg claimed they wanted only free speech when they burnt what they considered 'un-German' books (including the *Code Napoléon*) on their bonfires in 1817.

In peace and war German music continued to delight, enthral and inspire the whole of Europe. Weber and Schubert composed brilliant concertos, operas, symphonies and song-cycles, but the thundering talent of the age was that of Ludwig van Beethoven – perhaps the most famous German in history. For some, Beethoven's music was too revolutionary. For others, it was too difficult. When a violinist complained that Beethoven had presented him with a passage that was unplayable, he received the maestro's full wrath: 'When I composed that, I was conscious of being inspired by God Almighty. Do you think I can consider your puny little fiddle when He speaks to me?'

When the French Revolution threatened the life and safety of Louis XVI of France (*opposite, far right*), Friedrich Wilhelm II (*far left*) and Emperor Leopold II (*left*) met at Pillnitz (*above*).

Here, on 7 August 1791, they agreed to invade France if Louis was harmed. It was an empty threat, though one that gave false hope to the French royal family, including Charles, Duke of Artois (*right*), brother of Louis XVI and later Charles X of France. By April 1792 Prussia and Austria were at war with France.

Bonaparte's military triumphs in Germany sent shock waves through the empire. After his crushing defeat of the Austrians at the Battle of Austerlitz (*right*) on 2 December 1805, Pressburg, Bavaria and Württemberg became independent kingdoms. Within a year Bonaparte had set up the Confederation of the Rhine, and sixteen German states had joined, leaving the protection of the emperor. Prussia's attempt to form a rival North German Confederation was shattered by military defeats at Jena and Eylau (*far right, below*). (*Far right, above*) Carl von Clausewitz, who was captured by the French at Jena, but later became a staff officer in Blücher's army and wrote the 19th-century military textbook *Vom Kriege*.

(*Above*) A highly romanticised representation of Bonaparte accepting the Austrian surrender after the Battle of Austerlitz. (*Left*) The belligerent Emperor Franz II of Germany and Franz I of Austria, who joined almost every coalition against France – to little effect. (*Opposite, above*) The inaugural meeting of the Confederation of the Rhine. (*Opposite, below*) Two founder members of the Confederation – (*left*) Friedrich II of Württemberg, and (*right*) Maximilian Joseph I, King of Bavaria.

Eventually the fortunes of war changed. Gerhard Johann David von Scharnhorst (*above, left*) reformed the Prussian army, but died of wounds before he saw the fruits of his labour. On 16 October 1813, Bonaparte was defeated by an alliance of Austria, Prussia and Russia at the Battle of Leipzig.

(*Opposite, below*) The Emperor of Russia, King of Prussia and Emperor of Austria give thanks for victory on the battlefield of Leipzig. Gebhard Leberecht von Blücher, Prince of Wahlstadt (*opposite, above right*), took command of the Prussian army in the War of Liberation of 1813. The following year he invaded France and won a series of battles against Bonaparte. On Napoleon's return from Elba, Blücher once more commanded the Prussians and it was his timely arrival at Waterloo that ensured Bonaparte's final crushing defeat. (*Above*) Blücher and the Prussians on their way to Waterloo.

The Congress of Vienna, which met from 1814 to 1815, was an attempt to reform the structure and order of Germany. Prince Clemens Lothar Wenzel Metternich (*above, left*), the Austrian Foreign Minister, wished to see a German Federation under Austrian leadership, and the creation of a balance of power between Austria and Prussia. Prince Karl August von Hardenberg (*above, right*) was the leading Prussian statesman at the Congress. Although he broadly agreed with Metternich, he wanted Prussia to play a leading part in any German Federation.

Later, Hardenberg was responsible for many of the reforms of Prussia, including improvements in the army system, the abolition of serfdom and the privileges of the nobles, and improvements in education. (*Above*) The Congress in session. Seated on the far right is Charles Maurice de Talleyrand-Périgord, representative of the restored King Louis XVIII of France. Standing on the left is the British Duke of Wellington.

The fraternity of university students known as the *Burschenschaften* was one of the most vociferous
bodies calling for reform in Prussia at the end of the Napoleonic Wars. Students met, drank, debated
(*opposite*) and formulated their demands. They adopted the black, red and gold flag (later to be
adopted by all liberal nationalists). In October 1817, the Grand Duke Karl August von Sachsen-
Weimar-Eisenach gave permission for the students to hold their festival in the grounds of Wartburg
Castle (*above*). Copies of the *Code Napoléon* and the Prussian police laws were burnt. Calls were made
for national unity. But little was achieved.

(*Below, left*) A silhouette of Prince Wilhelm and Crown Prince Friedrich Wilhelm playing with toy soldiers in 1802. (*Left*) The meeting between Queen Luise of Prussia (second from left), Tsar Alexander I of Russia (third from left) and Friedrich Wilhelm III (third from right) at Memel. (*Below, right*) Queen Luise of Prussia. (*Opposite*) Karl Friedrich Schinkel's Babelsberg Palace.

The 1820s saw a flowering of German architecture, concentrated in Prussia on the works of Karl Friedrich Schinkel (*above, right*). Schinkel renovated many of the old palaces and hunting-lodges, in a style that was graceful and modern. (*Opposite, above*) The main façade of the Glienicke Palace, Berlin, rebuilt by Schinkel in 1827. (*Opposite, below and above, left*) The Tegel Palace, Berlin, another of Schinkel's reconstructions, built for the Humboldt family.

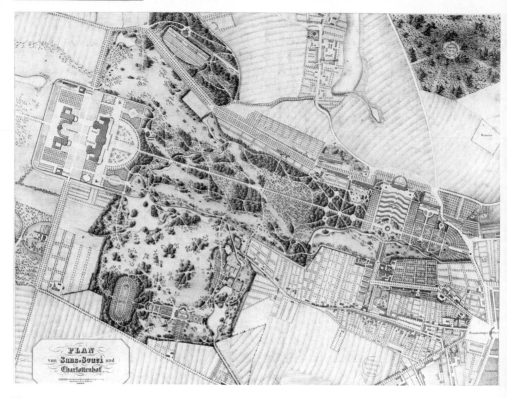

The great jewels of German architecture in the early 19th century were often magnificently set in the elaborately landscaped gardens that accompanied them. One of the most accomplished of those who 'improved' on nature was Peter Joseph Lenné (*opposite*), who had been recruited into the Prussian Landscape Gardening Department by Hardenberg at the Congress of Vienna. (*Above*) Lenné's design for the extension and improvement of the grounds of Sanssouci and Charlottenhof in January 1828.

In 1789 Carl Gotthard Langhans designed a new Brandenburg Gate (*right*) at the foot of Unter den Linden in Berlin, to replace the earlier Baroque design. Langhans was a classically trained architect who had already brought new architectural form to Berlin. The new gate was taller, more classical in design and consisted of six pairs of Doric columns supporting the main arch. To the sides were smaller wings that housed the guardhouse and the customs office.

The greatest musical creator of the age was Ludwig van Beethoven (*left*). In an incomparable body of work that included symphonies, concertos, sonatas, string quartets and the magnificent opera *Fidelio*, Beethoven rewrote the whole concept of musical form, harmony and exposition. Fighting encroaching deafness for much of his later life, Beethoven translated the whole canon of human emotions into musical terms. His legacy is unsurpassed. (*Below*) Beethoven's autograph. (*Opposite, below left*) A letter from Beethoven to his brother.

Carl Maria von Weber was a contemporary of Beethoven, a musical prodigy and the composer of at least two operas before he was fourteen. He was plagued by debt and dissipation for much of his short life, but managed to write three operatic masterpieces – *Der Freischütz* (1820), *Euryanthe* (1823), and *Oberon* (1826, the year of his death). (*Right*) Weber conducts *Der Freischütz* at London's Covent Garden in 1826. (*Below, right*) Jakob Ludwig Felix Mendelssohn-Bartholdy, c. 1830. Mendelssohn was a musical genius and another child prodigy – he gave his first piano recital at the age of nine. His brilliant and scintillating orchestral scores, songs and chamber works brought international fame.

Karl Wilhelm von Humboldt (*left*) was a diplomat and philologist, patron of the arts and sciences and an associate of Schiller. He was the first to study the Basque language, the founder of the Friedrich Wilhelm (later Humboldt) University of Berlin, and the first Minister of Education in Prussia. He was also Prussian Resident Minister in Rome from 1801 to 1808 (*opposite, below left*). Karl Wilhelm's younger brother, Alexander von Humboldt (*opposite, above left*), was a mineralogist and explorer. He spent many years in South America, visiting, among other places, La Paz, Bolivia (*opposite, above right*), and the Grand Temple of Vitsliputsli in Mexico (*opposite, below right*).

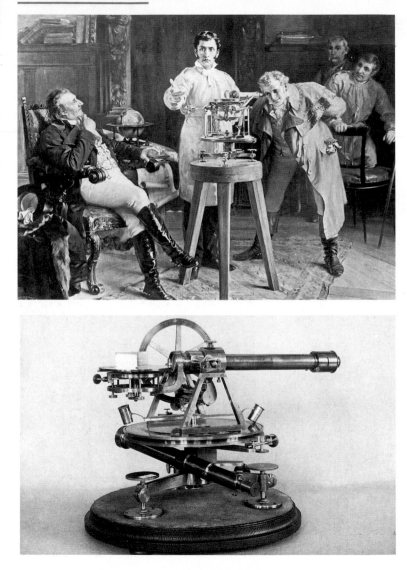

The advance of knowledge in Europe was led by German scientists in the early 19th century. Josef von Fraunhofer (*above, left*, in centre) invented the spectroscope (*below, left*), improved prisms and telescopes, and discovered the dark lines in the sun's spectrum – the Fraunhofer Lines. (*Opposite, clockwise from top left*) Georg Simon Ohm, who discovered the relationship between the strength of an unvarying electrical current, the electromotive force and the resistance of a circuit (Ohm's Law); Karl Friedrich Gauss, who invented the heliostat; Franz Josef Gall, who sought to establish the relationship between mental faculties and the shape of the skull (phrenology); and Friedrich Accum, who pioneered the use of gas lighting.

Caspar David Friedrich was the greatest of the German Romantic painters in the early 19th century. He saw the whole of nature, including the human soul, as evidence of the existence of the *Weltgeist* ('world spirit'). In most of his paintings, Friedrich places human beings in the foreground, in silhouette or dark colours, not as part of the landscape but merely as creatures that contemplate nature in all its wonder and horror. (*Right*) *Mann und Frau in Betrachtung des Mondes*, one of Friedrich's paintings dating from 1824, a period when his marriage to Caroline Bommer had temporarily lightened his spirit.

(*Above, left*) Friedrich von Schlegel, critic and philosopher and pioneer of the German Romantic movement. He led the movement against Bonaparte in 1809, but is best known for his philosophical works (*Philosophy of History, History of Philosophy* and *Philosophy of Life*). (*Above, right*) Friedrich's older brother, August Wilhelm von Schlegel, Professor of Literature at Jena University, and co-founder with his brother of the literary journal *Das Athenäum*. (*Opposite, above*) The Royal Theatre in Berlin. (*Opposite, below left*) Friedrich Ernst Daniel Schleiermacher, theologian and philosopher, and friend of the von Schlegels and von Humboldt. (*Opposite, below right*) The German poet and philosopher Johann Gottfried Herder.

(*Left*) Heinrich von Kleist, dramatist and poet, and author of the play *Prinz Friedrich von Homburg*. Kleist committed suicide in 1811 at the age of thirty-four. (*Above*) A meeting of a German literary circle in the early 19th century. (*Opposite, below right*) The German poet and novelist Wilhelm Hauff, whose simple fairy tales and short stories are full of fanciful delight. (*Opposite, below left*) Ernst Theodor Amadeus Hoffmann, archpriest of German High Romanticism. Hoffmann wrote a series of fantasies used by Offenbach as the basis for his *Tales of Hoffmann* and by Delibes as the story for *Coppelia*. (*Opposite, above*) An early 19th-century representation of Fairyland.

Introduction to Period 3 – 1825–2000

By the 1820s, a considerable body of influential Germans were eager to see a united, clearly defined and independent German state. The Romantics dreamed of a return to an idealalised medieval empire, indulging themselves in a *Deutschtümelei* – a glorification of all things German. The Liberals had hopes that a united Germany could become economically more powerful, with the abolition of internal trade barriers. Students and progressives wished to see a truly democratic Germany, with freedom of speech replacing the misery of censorship. The workers – who had not been consulted – wanted what they had always wanted: more food on the table, better housing and working conditions, and freedom from the misery of debt.

It was obvious that a newly unified Germany could never meet *all* these demands, but the present patchwork system had never been able to meet *any* of them. To that extent, unification had to be an improvement, and was inevitable. Within a short time, Germany was to become the centre of industrial capitalism – the most successful, the most efficient and the most competitive economy in the world. The tragedy was that this competitiveness was to be adopted by others within

Germany – by kings and chancellors, soldiers and right-wing nationalists – and within Austria, Britain, France and Russia.

In two brilliantly executed wars, the Prussian army attended the birth of Germany, like a brusque and expertly drilled midwife. It took just six weeks to inflict a humiliating defeat on Austria, and little more than a year to bring France to its knees. When Wilhelm I of Prussia was offered the hereditary crown of the new Germany in the Palace of Versailles on 18 January 1871, those whose approval echoed round the Hall of Mirrors were, almost to a man, soldiers or princes in uniform.

One of the few present who did not hold a military commission was Otto von Bismarck, Chancellor of the new Germany, a man with one of the wiliest if not wisest heads in Europe – and the man who had deliberately provoked the recent war with France. His creation was a three-layered German state. At the bottom was the *Reichstag*, a body directly elected by universal male suffrage and secret ballot. But its deputies received no pay, which made working-class representation impossible, and the *Reichstag* itself had little power. Above the *Reichstag* was the *Bundesrat* – a Federal

Council of delegates from the old German states, but completely dominated by Prussia. Real power was in the hands of those occupying the third layer (many of them to be seen in Anton von Werner's painting of the grand occasion in the Hall of Mirrors) – the Kaiser, the Chancellor, ministers, senior officials, and high-ranking officers in the army.

The new Germany was in many ways an imperfect creation, far removed from the dreams and wishes, demands and hopes of those that had worked and risked their lives for unity back in the 1830s and 1840s. But it was undeniably efficient. In the period from 1871 to 1914, the German population rose from 41 million to 67.7 million, an increase of almost 75 per cent; during the same period, the population of France rose by only 11 per cent. Industry developed at a staggering rate, particularly in the boom years of the 1890s, with the volume of German manufactured goods increasing by 400 per cent. In chemical and electrical industries, Germany led Europe, with only the United States as a serious (and distant) challenger.

Such achievements did little to endear Germany to its European neighbours. Wherever it appeared 19th-century nationalism was often jealous and xenophobic. It was all too easy for politicians to convince themselves and others that a nation's industrial energies were best channelled into arms production. In 1870 France had been able to offer little resistance to the weapons forged in the Krupps works at Essen. By 1900 Britain, France and Germany were all loudly calling for more ships, more guns, and more planes. But the more you had, the more you had to defend.

When the war came in 1914, Germany exhibited an exhausting display of brilliance, resilience, heroism, and sacrifice. When the crushingly harsh peace terms were foisted on to Germany, all that remained was bitterness. The country reeled out of the carnage into a mad dance of *Putsch* and counter-*Putsch*, with a feeling that there was unfinished business that would have to be attended to sooner or later.

The Depression that hit Germany in the 1920s was deeper, colder and darker than its grim manifestations in the rest of the world. Families were ruined. The young and the old starved to death. Children came home from school to discover that their desperate parents had committed suicide. Through this pain and tragedy a

grotesque humour often flickered. A tram ticket cost 100,000 marks, but a good seat in a theatre could be had for two eggs. One father sent his sons a wire which read: 'Dear boys, I am sending you 10 million Reichsmarks, so that you may at least enjoy a glass each of good Bavarian beer'! By the time the money arrived it wasn't enough for a thimbleful of beer.

Out of the darkness a new Germany marched into the nightmare of the Second World War. Bombed, battered, broken and carved into two states, the German people managed once again to pick themselves up and rebuild their land. More than that, they became the leading protagonists of a new Europe – an economic partnership that would abandon for ever the territorial greed and military rivalry that had cost millions of lives and brought the whole continent to its knees. The Iron and Steel Community, the Common Market and the EEC were all largely the creations of Germany and France.

West Germany became the capitalist showplace of Western Europe, with an economy that others envied and tried to emulate. East Germany – always the poor relation in the German family – became the socialist showplace of Eastern Europe, a land of cheap housing, low rents, and full employment, whose people envied West Germany and would have dearly loved the chance to emulate the miracle that had been wrought there.

In November 1989 the Berlin Wall was hacked to pieces, and Germany was once again united. Goethe would surely have approved.

11
REFORM AND REVOLUTION
1825–1848

The revolutionary year of 1848 was a time of confusion and chaos, of protest against existing governments throughout Germany and of Luddite violence against new machines and new factories. Liberals replaced reactionaries. Some princes abdicated, others temporarily withdrew. Street fighting in Vienna resulted in sixty deaths; in Berlin many more died. In fear, promises were made to abolish censorship, to convene parliaments, to adopt new constitutions. Some were kept. (*Right*) Troops under General von Prittwitz clear the Frankfurter Linden of protesters, 19 March 1848. Two hundred and thirty citizens were killed.

Introduction

Revolution and nationalism were growing side by side. Poets, writers, artists and intellectuals dreamed of a new Germany, and demanded the destruction of an antiquated system that was both inefficient and unjust. Just beyond the borders of Germany, the French renewed their revolutionary credentials in 1831. The poet and essayist Heinrich Heine was so moved by events there that he left Germany and went into voluntary exile, never to return. In 1841 Hoffmann von Fallersleben produced his patriotic and popular *Volkslieder*, which included *Deutschland, Deutschland über Alles*, later to become the German national anthem. But like so many revolutions, the impetus for action came from a shortage of food.

From 1843 to 1847 there was widespread famine throughout Germany. It was caused by a blight that destroyed most of the potato crop and by a succession of poor grain harvests. There were food riots in Vienna, Stuttgart and Ulm, and what amounted to a 'Potato Revolution' in Berlin.

Real wages dropped by more than 45 per cent. Worst hit were the Silesian linen-weavers. The German wool and cotton industries were strong enough to meet the challenge of British, French and Belgian imports. In Silesia, however, the feudal linen industry was beyond saving. Workers smashed looms and burnt the account books that listed their debts. The army restored order, but the plight of the weavers added fuel to the revolutionary flames that flickered all over Europe – some of them perhaps lit by 'Lucifers', the first matches, which made their appearance in Germany in 1829.

Faced with bitter unrest and an explosive situation, there was little that the rulers of Germany could do – even if they had wanted to. Friedrich Wilhelm IV of Prussia was possessed by vague and outmoded ideas of the divine right of kings. Ludwig I of Bavaria was a lavish-spending reactionary who was more interested in Lola Montez, an Irish dancer from County Limerick. Franz II of Austria (last of the Holy Roman emperors) was popular but inherently conservative. All were remnants from the age of absolutism, knowing little of the events confronting authority – least of all how to control them.

Germany erupted in 1848. In March reactionaries in many assemblies were replaced by liberals, in the hope that a little change would suffice. Moderate governments were created in Baden, Württemberg, Hanover, Saxony and other, smaller, states. Ludwig of Bavaria abdicated in favour of his son. It wasn't enough.

Sixty people were killed when street fighting broke out in Vienna. At least two hundred and thirty were killed in Berlin when troops were ordered to disperse an orderly crowd. Three days later Friedrich Wilhelm rode through the city, announcing: 'I do not want to rule, I want Germany's freedom, Germany's unity...I swear to God.'

A generation later his wishes came true.

In January 1834 eighteen German states, under Prussian auspices, formed a customs union (*Zollverein*). One of the leading proponents was Friedrich List (*opposite*). Other leaders included (*below,* left to right) Friedrich von Motz, Karl Georg von Maasen, Wilhelm von Klewiz and Friedrich von Eichhorn. (*Right*) The *Zollverein* meets at Crystal Palace, 1851.

(*Right*) The opening of the first German railway, which linked Nuremberg with Fürth, on 7 December 1835. Although some ten years behind Britain, development of the German railway network was swift. Within a few years, Germany had the most extensive railway system on the continent of Europe. The ability to move large quantities of iron, coal, steel and manufactured goods swiftly about the country did much to accelerate the German industrial revolution.

Ludwig I of Bavaria spent lavishly on paintings, public buildings, Court favourites and Lola Montez
(*below, left*), a dancer from Limerick in Ireland. Ludwig's son Ludwig II (*above, left*), was similarly profli-
gate, though his passion was for castle-building on a grand scale. The castles of Linderhof (*above, right*)
and Neuschwanstein (*opposite*) between them cost 15 million guilden, while the attempt to build a copy
of Versailles at Herrenchiemsee was even more expensive.

1847, the year preceding the Revolution, was a year of violent action in Germany. There were riots in more than one hundred towns, the worst of which were concentrated in Prussia and Silesia. A blight which destroyed much of the potato crop in Germany and a failure of the grain harvest led to the Potato Revolution in Berlin. Bread shops were looted (*opposite*) in April. (*Above*) A scene of desolation and suffering in a Silesian weaver's cottage. Wages were halved in the 1840s. Food was scarce. Hours and conditions of work were appalling. (*Right*) A much depleted market in Ulm during the 1840s.

Friedrich Wilhelm IV was a confused man. Although he promised reform, he believed in the divine right of kings and opposed the notion of popular government. Like most German rulers, he was unaware of the strength of feeling of the people he ruled. (*Left*) Revolutionaries meet in a Berlin cellar, 1848.

Friedrich Wilhelm's hand was forced by the events of March 1848. Despite merciless attacks by armed troops, thousands of citizens stormed the Prince's palace in Berlin (*opposite, above*), and the Royal Arsenal (*above*). On 19 March Friedrich Wilhelm ordered his troops to leave the city. Two days later he rode through Berlin declaring that he no longer wished to rule, and that all he wanted was Germany's freedom and Germany's unity. On the same day he issued a proclamation which included the incomprehensible phrase: 'henceforth Prussia merges into Germany'. It was taken as a sign that the Revolution had been successful.

On 1 May 1848 elections were held in Prussia for the National Assembly and for the Frankfurt parliament. Within three weeks three hundred and fifty delegates had been elected and the parliament formally opened in Paulskirche, Frankfurt (*above, right*). Friedrich Wilhelm IV (*above, left*) contemplated this change with neither enthusiasm nor fury. The Prussian monarchy was still reeling from the effects of the riots of March. Prince Wilhelm had fled to London. Bismarck had yet to take the centre stage of history.

Nevertheless, Germany effectively now had a new government. The parliament chamber, inside the Paulskirche (*above*), was packed with an odd assortment of interests, classes and personalities. The Frankfurt parliament was recognised by Sweden, the Netherlands, Switzerland, Belgium and the United States, but – significantly – not by Russia, France or Britain. It had no executive power, no constitution and no money. Most seriously, it was divided in opinion on every key issue.

One of Friedrich Wilhelm IV's more exotic creations was the Engine House (*above, right*) in the grounds of the Palace of Sanssouci. It housed machinery to pump water from the River Havel to the fountains in the park, and was designed by Ludwig Persius. Work began in 1841 and took two years to complete. (*Above, left*) Friedrich Wilhelm IV, c. 1840. (*Opposite*) A view inside the Engine House, with the spiral staircase leading up to the ornate dome. The richness of decoration rivals that of a mosque.

The parade of exceptional musical talent in German culture continued into the mid-19th century. Robert and Clara Schumann (*above, left and right*) both composed wonderful music for the piano, for chamber ensembles and for the voice. Clara Schumann was also a pianist of the highest class. (*Left*) Twelve bars in canon form of Robert Schumann's *Ritornelles* for male chorus.

The genius of Franz Schubert (*right*) blazed for a pitifully short time, for he died at the age of thirty-one. In his brief life, however, he wrote nine symphonies, twenty-one piano sonatas and some of the finest songs in musical history. (*Below, right*) The musical manuscript of Schubert's song *Erlkönig* (Erl King). Changes on the manuscript show that the use of triplets in the right-hand accompaniment was an afterthought. Both Schumann and Schubert were regular frequenters of the coffee houses popular among German artists at this time – Schumann favouring Poppe's Kaffeebaum, Schubert favouring Bogner's.

The Prince Maximilian zu Wied (*left*) was a German naturalist and traveller who spent much of his time in North America. He compiled a journal (*below*) which recorded the flora and fauna, and the customs and costumes of the tribes that he met. He was accompanied by the artist Karl Bodmer, whose illustrations greatly enhanced the writings of Maximilian. (*Opposite*) Three paintings by Karl Bodmer dating from 1833 and 1834. (*Opposite, above*) A group of Mandans crossing a frozen lake. (*Opposite, below left*) Péhriska-Rúhpa, a Hidatsa warrior, performing the Dog Dance. (*Opposite, below right*) A young Omaha boy.

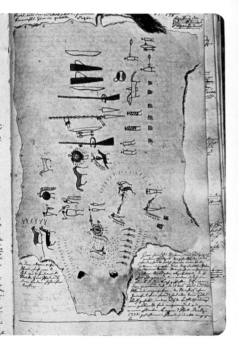

Justus Freiherr von Liebig (*above, left*) was one of the greatest experimental chemists of the early 19th century. At the age of twenty-one he became Professor of Chemistry at Giessen, where many of his experiments came to fruition. He was the founder of agricultural chemistry and one of the discoverers of chloroform and its properties. (*Below, left*) A cloth soaked in chloroform is held over the patient's face in an operating theatre of the 1870s. Liebig was best known to ordinary people, however, as the inventor of Liebig's Meat Extract.

Friedrich Wöhler (*left*) became Professor of Chemistry at Göttingen in 1836, by which time he had already isolated aluminium and beryllium, and revolutionised organic chemistry by synthesising urea from ammonium cyanate. (*Above*) The first practical teaching laboratory in the world, established by Justus von Liebig at Giessen. Here Liebig introduced methods of analysing carbon and hydrogen, manufactured potassium cyanide and worked with Wöhler on the properties of uric acid.

While liberals and conservatives clashed, and workers and employers fought, rival philosophers argued and questioned the theories advanced by others. Artur Schopenhauer (*left*) found inspiration in the works of Plato, and bitterly opposed the work of Georg Wilhelm Friedrich Hegel (*opposite, below right*) and Friedrich Schelling (*opposite, below left*). Between them these three intellectual giants revolutionised thinking throughout the world. All three taught at Jena University (*opposite, above*). Hegel lived and taught in Frankfurt (*above*), the city to which Schopenhauer retired and where he lived out his life as a recluse, accompanied only by his pet poodle.

(*Above, left*) Heinrich Heine, German poet and essayist who was born in Dusseldorf (*left*) in 1797. Heine's poems were an instant success when published from the 1820s onwards. (*Above, right*) Gustav Herold's statue of the Rhine maiden known as the Lorelei, the subject of one of Heine's most famous poems.

(*Above, left*) Georg Büchner, German dramatist and pioneer of Expressionist theatre. He was the author of the poetic drama *Woyzeck*, later used by Alban Berg as the basis for his opera *Wozzeck*. (*Above, right*) Johann Christian Friedrich Hölderlin, one of greatest German poets of all time. (*Right*) Tübingen-am-Neckar, where Hölderlin lived for most of his life.

Heidelberg (*opposite, above right*) became the centre of one of the most powerful and successful schools of German Romantic poets. Among their number were Bettina von Arnim (*opposite, above left*) and her brother Clemens von Bretano (*opposite, below left*). (*Opposite, below right*) Joseph Freiherr von Eichendorff, poet and novelist best remembered for his romantic lyric poetry. (*Right*) The Baroness Annette Elisabeth von Droste-Hülshoff, reckoned by many to be Germany's finest woman writer. She was in many ways more restrained than the Romantic poets, though her work was much influenced by Byron.

One hundred and fifty years after their deaths, Jakob Ludwig and Wilhelm Karl Grimm (*left*, Jakob is wearing the cap) are remembered as collectors and re-tellers of the most popular fairy and folk tales in the world. They were also philologists and politicians, both of them being dismissed from professorships at Göttingen University for refusing to take the oath of allegiance to the King of Prussia. (*Below, left and right*) Two of their most famous fairy tales – *Cinderella* and *Little Red Riding Hood*. (*Opposite*) *German Fairy Tales in Words and Pictures*, the title page to *Snow White*. 'What would youth be without fairy tales...'

Deutſche Märchen in Wort und Bild.
2
Schneeweißchen.

Widmung.

Was wärſt du ſchöne Jugendzeit
Denn ohne Märchenblüthen?
Wenn ſie nicht goldnen Sternen gleich
An deinem himmel glühten.

Ein Jugendmorgen ohne ſie
Er wäre halbes Leben;
Du glücklich Kind, dem ſie den Lenz
Der Jugend hold umſchweben.

Gewiß man ſagt es unbewußt:
„Das Märchen ſei nur Lüge;"
Es iſt des Kindes reinſte Luſt,
Des Kindergeiſtes Wiege.

Gedeih'! du ewig grüner Baum
Streu deinen Blüthenſegen
Der goldnen Jugend in den Schooß
Wie einen Zauberregen.

Frankfurt am Main
Verlag von
E. G. May Söhne.

Friedrich Wilhelm August Froebel (*left*) was the founder of the *Kindergarten* education system – seeking to help a child's mind develop naturally and spontaneously. His methods and ideas spread rapidly, and Froebel-inspired schools were opened throughout Europe (*opposite, below*). Heinrich Hoffmann was similarly unimpressed by traditional provision made for children. He described children's books of the early 19th century as 'altogether too enlightened and rational, falsely naive, unchildlike, untruthful, artificial...' So he wrote *Struwwelpeter* (*opposite, above*), a vividly illustrated book that showed children what would happen to them if they sucked their thumbs, played with matches, failed to look where they were going, etc...

(*Above*) A caricature of the working of censorship in Hanover in 1837. It depicts the new king, Ernst August, brother of William IV of Britain. One of his first acts was to exile the seven professors of Göttingen University. When Ernst August's attack on the constitution of 1833 was debated in the Bundestag, only Bavaria, Saxony, Württemberg, Baden and the Saxon duchies opposed him. The Federation lost all credibility.

12
THE UNIFICATION OF GERMANY 1849–1871

The Krupp dynasty forged the weapons that procured German
unification. Friedrich Krupp founded a small iron forge in Essen
in 1810, where his son Alfred began manufacturing arms in
1837. Within ten years the factory supplied weapons to countries
all over the world. Alfred built up a vast industrial empire,
owning mines, collieries and docks, and extending the Krupp
factories and workshops in the Ruhr valley to become the arsenal
of the Prussian army. (*Right*) Interior of the Krupp steelworks at
Essen, c. 1870.

Introduction

The revolutions of 1848 did little to bring about the unification of Germany or to solve the social and political problems inherent in the old empire. Liberals and democrats, progressives and radicals decided that it was more constructive to work within the system than to attempt to overthrow it.

Nationalist sentiment smouldered. There was much to be proud of in mid-19th-century Germany. For the ear, there were the music-dramas of Wagner, the symphonies of Brahms, and the virtuosity of Liszt; for the eye, the boulevards of Berlin (of which the finest was Unter den Linden) and the fashionable charm of Baden-Baden. For the mind, there were the writings of Schopenhauer, and the dramas of Hebbel and Freytag. And for the pocket, there were the wonders of the Berlin Stock Exchange.

For those who wished to see a united Germany, it seemed that the task ahead was ever more complex. There was no point in establishing a new confederation under the old hegemony of Austria. There were grave dangers in allowing Prussia to take the lead. Most German princes, and millions of others, were appalled by Bismarck's remarks to the *Landtag*, delivered shortly after he had been appointed head of government by Wilhelm I. 'The great questions of the day,' he declared, 'are not decided by speeches and majority votes, which were the great mistakes of 1848 and 1849, but by blood and iron.' Here was Prussian militarism at its most grotesque.

But Bismarck was the one man determined to create a clear way ahead, even if none was visible. Using diplomacy that owed much to Machiavelli at his most cunning, Bismarck ran rings round the Emperor Franz Joseph and his Habsburg advisers. Issue after issue was resolved in Prussia's favour, and when it came to a showdown the Prussian army crushed the might of Austria with contemptuous ease. It was now proposed that Germany should be divided into three separate parts – northern (which included Hanover, Hessen, Nassau, Frankfurt and the newly acquired territories of Schleswig-Holstein), southern (Bavaria, Baden, Württemberg and Hessen-Darmstadt), and Austria (licking its wounds and seeking comfort in the waltzes of the Strauss family).

Man proposed, Bismarck disposed. It was time to turn his attention to the war he was anticipating (if not planning) with France. Disgruntled Germans complained that Bismarck's motto for the country was 'Pay taxes, shut your trap, and become a soldier!' They were almost certainly right, for in Bismarck's eyes war was the tool with which to fashion the new Germany. The Prussian army took 100,000 French prisoners at the Battle of Sedan, and four months later Wilhelm I was proclaimed Emperor of Germany.

Franz Josef I (*above, left*), Emperor of Austria from 1848 to 1916, spent most of his long reign seeking to hold his disparate empire together. The Habsburg hold on Germany had steadily diminished, and Franz Josef looked increasingly to the east as the basis for his power. Here he found nothing but trouble – Hungarian moves for independence, European opposition to the initiatives he took in the Balkans, and eventually, war with Serbia. (*Above, right*) The Empress Elisabeth Emelie Eugene in 1854. She was the wife of the Emperor Franz Josef, an unhappy woman, who was fatally stabbed by an anarchist in Geneva in 1898.

Wilhelm I (*above, left*) was King of Prussia from 1861 and Emperor of Germany from 1871 to 1888. His reign was marked by a succession of wars, through all of which the Prussian army acquitted itself with breathtaking success. Wilhelm was greatly aided by Bismarck throughout his reign, for the emperor was a modest and unassuming man who lacked the diplomatic skills necessary to guide Germany through one of the most exciting and unsettled periods in its history. (*Above, right*) The Princess Augusta of Saxe-Weimar, wife of Wilhelm I and Empress of Germany.

(*Opposite*) Prince Otto Edward Leopold von Bismarck, the Iron Chancellor and arbiter of Prussian and German fortunes for much of the second half of the 19th century – a photograph taken in 1860. Bismarck was fervently royalist, consumed with the notion of German unification, and a man who believed in war as a necessary political and diplomatic tool. (*Right*) Bismarck (on the right) with his pack of hounds. (*Below, left*) A drawing by Gustave von Kessel of the nineteen-year-old Bismarck, then a student at Göttingen University. (*Below, right*) Bismarck with the actress Pauline Lucca. The photographer who took this picture was jailed for six months, and it was falsely claimed that the photo was a fake.

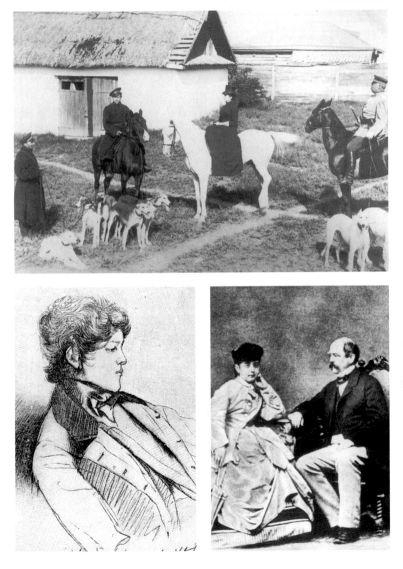

Socialism reared its disruptive head in many parts of Germany in the later 19th century, though those who preached this new gospel received short shrift from the authorities. Wilhelm Liebknecht (*opposite, above left*, with Tussy Marx, daughter of Karl Marx) was imprisoned for his left-wing views. August Ferdinand Bebel (*opposite, below left*) was leader of the German Social Democratic movement. Ferdinand Lassalle (*opposite, right*) was a political journalist and champion of the working class. (*Left*) A Walter Crane illustration from *Kulturbilde, die Hohenzollern – Legende,* depicting the solidarity of the proletariat.

The development of the railway network was an important factor in creating the economic and industrial success that aided the movement for German unity. Railways boosted the stock market, supplied industry with raw materials, hurried goods to market, and served as troop carriers. (*Opposite*) The Tauern railway in Carinthia. (*Above, right*) The early steam locomotive *Kopernicus* in 1858. (*Below, right*) The Stadtbahn in Alexanderplatz, Berlin. 'It was always a hell of a place,' wrote one Berliner, '...there was never much point in going that far east in the city...'

In 1851 Alfred Krupp (*left*) produced the world's first cannon made of pure steel. This, and millions of other products from the works at Essen, played a considerable part in shaping Prussian foreign policy over the next twenty years. (*Opposite, above right*) The Krupp works in Essen, 1861. In the foreground is the building that housed the original blacksmith's forge of Alfred's father Friedrich. (*Opposite, above left*) The first private artillery practice ground in the world, joined by railway to the Krupp works. (*Opposite, below*) The Krupp works in 1850. Alfred Krupp was in many ways a model employer, giving his workers sick pay, free medical treatment, pensions and retirement homes.

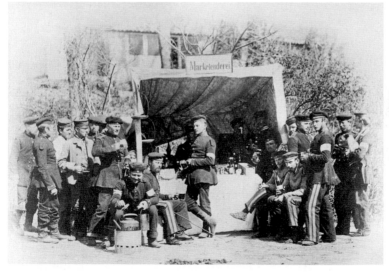

Prussia's first trial of military strength came in the war with Denmark, from February to October 1864. Weapons and tactics were similar to those of the American Civil War, though the fighting lasted nothing like as long. The cause of the war was Denmark's claim to the province of Schleswig, the majority of whose population was German.

A series of photographs by Henry Guttmann of the war between the Austro-Prussian alliance and Denmark. (*Opposite, above left*) German sentries on the ruins of the Danish fortress of Düppel. (*Opposite, above right*) A photograph taken just after the storming of Danish defences at Düppel by Prussian troops under Prince Friedrich Karl. (*Opposite, below*) A Prussian army canteen at Gravenstein. (*Above, right*) A section of the 3rd Brandenburg Jäger battalion at the Battle of Oster Düppel, 18 April 1864. (*Right, below*) Army smiths working on the garrison vehicle park at Nubelfeld.

The Austro-Prussian alliance was sacrificed by Bismarck to save his tottering political career. On 8 April 1866 Prussia signed an alliance with Austria's enemy Italy. Two months later war began. (*Opposite, above left*) Count Helmuth von Moltke, the man who rebuilt the Prussian army. (*Opposite, above right*) Some of the soldiers in von Moltke's new force. (*Opposite, below*) A cavalry skirmish during the Austro-Prussian War. (*Below, right*) The battlefield of Sadowa, 3 July 1866, scene of Austria's crushing defeat. (*Above, right*) The Crown Prince of Prussia visits wounded troops after Sadowa.

Many obstacles still stood in the way of German unification – the split between Catholics and Protestants, opposition from France and Austria, and anti-Prussian feeling in Germany. In the spring of 1870, the Spanish parliament offered the throne of Spain to a member of the Catholic branch of the Prussian ruling family. France objected. War broke out on 19 July 1870.

(*Opposite, above*) The moment of glory. Prussian troops pose on their artillery in the Place de la Concorde after marching into Paris. (*Opposite, below*) German soldiers enjoy a cigarette during a break from laying down telegraph lines. When war was declared, one French commander reported that the French army was in a chamber pot 'about to be shitted upon'. He was right. The defeat of France was swift and ignominious. (*Above*) Prussian troops at Fort Issy, one of the strategic defence posts on the outskirts of Paris, 31 January 1871. The Armistice had been signed three days earlier.

During the occupation of Paris, the Prussian army gave several spectacular displays of its military power. (*Above*) Prussian horse artillery photographed by Guttmann early in 1871. (*Opposite, above*) The remains of the town of Bazeilles, near the battlefield of Sedan in Grande Champagne. Sedan was the greatest of the Prussian victories. More than 100,000 prisoners were taken, including the Emperor Napoleon III. (*Opposite, below*) The Hall of Mirrors in the Palace of Versailles, converted into a German hospital during the Franco-Prussian War.

(*Opposite*) A caricature of a German soldier covering the former French provinces of Alsace and Lorraine with Prussian blue paint after they had been surrendered to Germany. (*Above*) In a painting by Wilhelm Camphausen, Chancellor Bismarck talks with his prisoner Napoleon III on the morning after the French surrender at Sedan. (*Right*) Wilhelm I is proclaimed Emperor of Germany in the Palace of Versailles, 18 January 1871.

Views of four of Germany's most prosperous cities in the latter part of the 19th century. (*Above*) Old houses line the end of the canal in Hamburg. In the 1880s there were widespread strikes here when these houses were demolished to make way for the *Speicherstadt,* the port's tax-free warehouses. (*Left*) The centre of Dresden, September 1868. The cathedral is the largest church in Saxony and was commissioned by the Elector Friedrich August II in the late 1730s.

(*Above, right*) The Rhine at Cologne, c. 1870. The cathedral is clearly distinguished by its two spires, but was as yet still unfinished. The English author of *Alice in Wonderland*, Lewis Carroll, described it as 'the most beautiful of all the churches I have ever seen.... If one could imagine the spirit of devotion embodied in any material form, it would be in such a building...' (*Below, right*) The old port of Stettin on the Baltic. It had been an eastern bulwark of the German people for hundreds of years.

The healing qualities of the hot springs in the Florintinerberg at Baden-Baden had been known to the Romans. Over a thousand years later the Swiss alchemist and doctor Paracelsus had used them to save the life of the Margrave Philippe I. But it was to Napoleon Bonaparte that the spa town owed its increasing good fortune in the 19th century.

(*Opposite, above*) The town and surroundings of Baden-Baden.
(*Opposite, below*) A typical example of the grand villas built at
Baden-Baden in the mid-19th century. From the 1840s to the
1860s, the Casino founded in Baden-Baden by the French
impresario Jacques Benazet (*Le Roi de Baden*) attracted many
visitors. (*Above*) The Kurhaus of Baden-Baden, built by Friedrich
Weinbrenner. (*Right*) A bridge across the rocks overlooking
Baden-Baden in the late 19th century.

The mid-19th century saw the development of some of the greatest names in German industry, among them the Siemens family. Ernst Werner von Siemens (*above, left*) and his brother Karl Wilhelm von Siemens (*above, right*). The company was founded by Ernst in 1844 and became known as the Siemens Brothers in 1867.

(*Opposite, below*) The miniature electrically powered train made by Siemens for the Berlin Trade Fair of 1879. Siemens made gutta percha, telegraphic apparatus and equipment, and dynamos. (*Above*) The Siemens system tram, invented by Karl Wilhelm in the 1860s. (*Right*) The Siemens steel smelting furnace, which used an open hearth and became the most common form of furnace in the world.

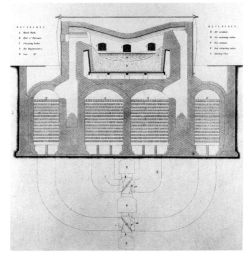

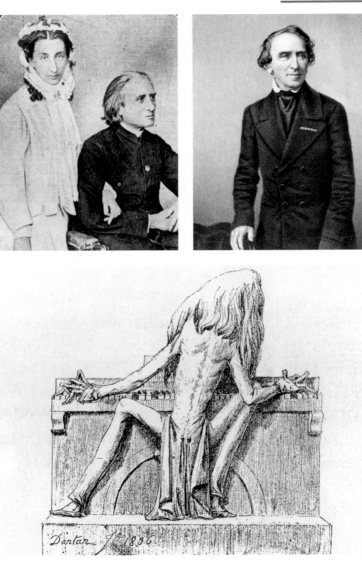

.and still they came. The German domination of classical music continued with the age of Johannes Brahms (*opposite, below left*), Franz Liszt and Giacomo Meyerbeer (formerly Jakob Beer) (*above, right*). (*Opposite, above*) The Gewandhaus Hall in Leipzig, where Mendelssohn was resident conductor from 1835 to 1847, and where Liszt was a frequent performer. (*Above, left*) The Hungarian composer and pianist Franz Liszt with his daughter Cosima, later to become the wife of Richard Wagner. (*Below*) A caricature of Liszt playing the piano, dating from the late 19th century.

The industrial revolution gathered pace in Germany throughout the 19th century. The railway system, hard-surfacing of roads, canals and the introduction of steamships on the Rhine helped the process. One of the pioneers of the new industrial age was August Borsig (*opposite*), who built a vast iron-rolling works and locomotive manufacturing factory in Berlin-Moabit (*above*) in the 1840s and 1850s.

(*Right*) The Friedrichs-
brücke over the River
Spree in the heart of
Berlin at the end of the
19th century. The
building on the bank of
the river is the Berlin
Stock Exchange, designed
by Friedrich Hitzig and
built between 1859 and
1864. Although the
building was imposing,
the work done inside it
was not impressive.
Reformers claimed that
this was because the Stock
Exchange was burdened
by too many regulations
and too much stamp
duty. Kaiser Wilhelm II
described the system as
'idiotic'.

13
THE PILOT
1871–1890

The German aeronautical engineer and pioneer of heavier-than-air flight, Otto Lilienthal. He was born in Anklam in 1849, and was killed when one of his gliders crashed near Berlin in 1896. Many of his glider designs were based on the sketches of Leonardo da Vinci. In the machines that he built himself, Lilienthal made hundreds of short flights, blazing a trail for the Wright brothers, Blériot and many German pilots.

Introduction

It was all too much for one man. Bismarck's attempts to act as puppet-master of Europe ultimately failed. The stage was too big, the puppets too wilful, and there was so much at stake. The entire Western world was locked in a race for new territories, new markets, and new industries in the last decades of the 19th century. To the east, Russia and the Ottoman Turks locked antlers to decide the fate of Serbia, Bosnia, Bulgaria and Montenegro. To the west, there were threatening alliances between Britain and France. Abroad, there were Germany's new-found colonies in Africa, New Guinea and the Pacific islands to be protected, nourished, exploited. At home, Bismarck had to deal with the Marxists, the ADAV (General German Workers' Association) and the Social Democrat Party (SPD).

That he lasted so long is a tribute to Bismarck's skill and cunning. The end came in

1890 when the *Reichstag* elections resulted in a defeat for his cartel of liberals and conservatives. Bismarck considered overthrowing the constitution, but he had run out of allies. His resignation was accepted with relief (and thanks) by the young Kaiser Wilhelm II. The pilot was dropped, though Wilhelm announced that 'the course remains the same, full steam ahead!'

Industrially, Germany outstripped the rest of Europe. AEG and Siemens were established by the 1870s. Gottlieb Daimler produced one of the earliest motor cars in 1885 and founded the Daimler-Motoren-Gesellschaft five years later. The electric tram came to Berlin 1881, electric lighting and general power in 1884. Rudolf Diesel began his pioneering work on the internal combustion engine. Otto Lilienthal took the art and science of gliding to new heights.

Berlin became one of the most elegant cities in the world. Cologne Cathedral was at last finished – though not to the satisfaction of the locals, who promptly built the main railway station as close as possible to it. Gustav Mahler wrote the first of his ten symphonies. Anton Bruckner wrote all but the last of his nine symphonies. These and other great works were played by the newly formed Berlin Philharmonic Orchestra. Leopold von Ranke wrote the greatest of his historical works, and Nietzsche wrote *Also sprach Zarathustra* and *Jenseits von Gut und Böse*. Meanwhile, in the Reading Room of the British Museum, Karl Marx completed *Das Kapital*, the 19th-century handbook of socialism.

Less revolutionary, but just as long-lasting, were the advertising pillars invented by Litfass, and the world's first teddy bears, made by Steiff.

(*Left*) Wilhelm I, seventh King of Prussia and first Emperor of Germany, with his wife, Princess Augusta of Saxe-Weimar, c. 1880. He died in 1888 and was succeeded by his only son, Friedrich III (*opposite, above left*, with his family). Friedrich was a liberal who protested against the reactionary policies of Bismarck. However, he died of throat cancer within a year of coming to the throne. (*Opposite, below*) The funeral of Friedrich III in June 1888. Friedrich was succeeded by his son, Wilhelm II, who loved military splendour, flirted with the divine right of kings, and whose quickness of intellect was matched by his temper. (*Opposite, above right*) Wilhelm II with his son, the Crown Prince Wilhelm, Potsdam, 1887.

The Iron Chancellor had controlled German fortunes for almost thirty years. (*Opposite, above*) Bismarck addresses the German *Reichstag*, c. 1880. (*Opposite, below*) Bismarck (centre) with his deputies Count Lerchenfeld (right) and Freiherr von Strengel (left). Bismarck's control did not last long after the succession of Wilhelm II. The new Kaiser had sworn to oust Bismarck and take control himself. (*Above, right*) The famous cartoon showing Wilhelm 'dropping the pilot', from *Punch* magazine, 29 March 1890. (*Right*) A letter from Bismarck to Lord Rosebery, acknowledging birthday congratulations. (*Above, left*) Bismarck leaves his house by carriage.

Wilhelm I shared his grandson's pride in the Prussian and German armies. He strengthened Prussian forces to consolidate his own power and to place Prussia in a position to lead Germany. (*Above*) Wilhelm drives to military manoeuvres in his carriage. (*Left*) German cavalry and infantry practise their skills, 1883.

(*Above*) German soldiers on parade during the reign of Wilhelm I. (*Right*) One of the very first German submarines, photographed by Henry Guttmann in 1855. The boat had failed to surface and had been hauled from the bottom of the harbour in Kiel.

In the late 19th century, France, Britain and Germany scrambled for control of the African continent. German influence was strongest in East Africa, where German engineers built railways to link their provinces. (*Above*) Constructing the line between Dar es Salaam and Morogoro. German initiatives were less successful in southern Africa, where their ally Paul Kruger (*opposite, above left*), President of the Transvaal, lost to the British. Two pictures by Reinhold Thiele from the Boer War: (*opposite, above right*) German medical officers, and (*opposite, below*) a hospital ward run by the German Red Cross during the Boer War.

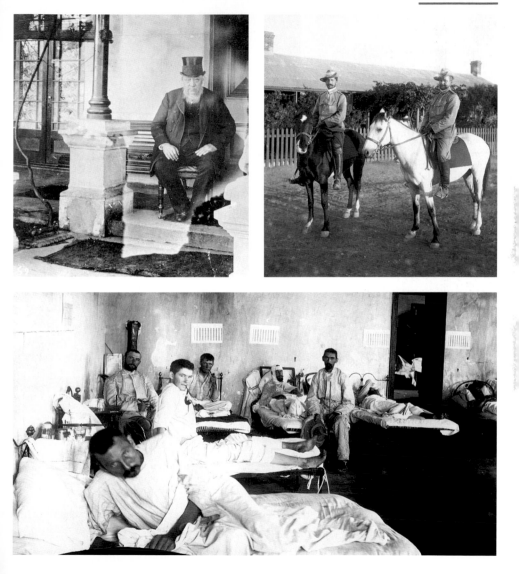

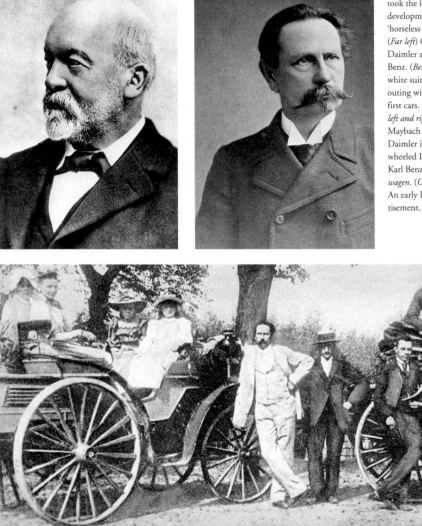

German motor engineers took the lead in the development of the 'horseless carriage'. (*Far left*) Gottlieb Daimler and (*left*) Karl Benz. (*Below*) Benz, in white suit, on a family outing with one of his first cars. (*Opposite, above left and right*) Wilhelm Maybach and Paul Daimler in the first four-wheeled Daimler car, and Karl Benz in his *Dreiradwagen*. (*Opposite, below*) An early Daimler advertisement.

Robert Koch (*left*) was a German physician and bacteriologist whose work on wounds, septicaemia and splenic fever earned him a place on the imperial Board of Health in 1880. In 1883 he travelled to Egypt and India, where he succeeded in isolating the cholera bacteria. The following year Koch was able to demonstrate cholera bacilli at the German Exhibition (*opposite, below*). He was rewarded by the German government for the work he had done and went on to be awarded the Nobel Prize for Medicine in 1905.

During his life, Koch was seen as an international hero. (*Above, right*) A British portrait of Robert Koch as St George, slayer of the tuberculosis dragon, though his work in this field was less successful. (*Above, left*) A contemporary caricature of the precautions to be taken against cholera. The woman carries a smoking vessel (to protect her from foul air) and wears hot-water bottles on her feet to protect her from fever.

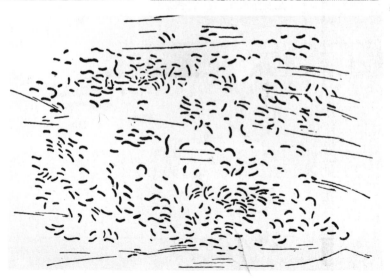

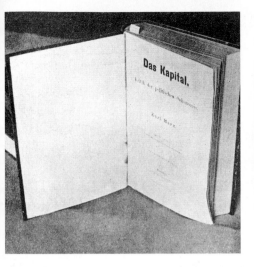

Perhaps the most influential book of the entire 19th century was *Das Kapital* (*above, left*) by the German social, political and economic theorist Karl Marx (*opposite*), photographed by Henry Guttmann. Marx's analysis of the structure and future of capitalism was partly based on observation. He had seen the struggles of the poor to earn a living in the mid-19th century, such as the women who sold old clothes in German street markets (*above, right*). (*Right*) The co-founder, with Marx, of scientific socialism, Friedrich Engels, photographed by Edward Gooch in 1860.

(*Left*) Adolph von Menzel's heroic painting of the heat and sweat of *The Rolling-Mill*, depicting the immense energy and effort of German industry in the tumultuous years of the 1870s. The Franco-Prussian War was over. Germany was at last united. What was needed was a powerful industrial base from which to challenge the rest of the world. Von Menzel specialised in painting historical pictures of the times of Friedrich the Great, but he also recorded scenes of fashionable life in his own times, and the work of the masses during the reign of Wilhelm I.

(*Left*) The vast factory floor at AEG, Berlin, in 1890. The machines in production are turbine engines. (*Top*) The first diesel motor built by Krupp Industries. It ran for over forty years. (*Above*) A workshop of the Boehringer Company in Mannheim, 1885.

— 73 —

Reichs-Gesetzblatt.

№ 9.

Inhalt: Gesetz, betreffend die Krankenversicherung der Arbeiter. S. 73.

(Nr. 1496.) Gesetz, betreffend die Krankenversicherung der Arbeiter. Vom 15. Juni 1883.

Wir Wilhelm, von Gottes Gnaden Deutscher Kaiser, König von Preußen ꝛc.

verordnen im Namen des Reichs, nach erfolgter Zustimmung des Bundesraths und des Reichstags, was folgt:

A. Versicherungszwang.

§ 1.

Personen, welche gegen Gehalt oder Lohn beschäftigt sind:

1. in Bergwerken, Salinen, Aufbereitungsanstalten, Brüchen und Gruben, in Fabriken und Hüttenwerken, beim Eisenbahn- und Binnendampfschifffahrtsbetriebe, auf Werften und bei Bauten,

2. im Handwerk und in sonstigen stehenden Gewerbebetrieben,

3. in Betrieben, in denen Dampfkessel oder durch elementare Kraft (Wind, Wasser, Dampf, Gas, heiße Luft ꝛc.) bewegte Triebwerke zur Verwendung kommen, sofern diese Verwendung nicht ausschließlich in vorübergehender Benutzung einer nicht zur Betriebsanlage gehörenden Kraftmaschine besteht,

sind mit Ausnahme der im §. 2 unter Ziffer 2 bis 6 aufgeführten Personen, sofern nicht die Beschäftigung ihrer Natur nach eine vorübergehende oder durch den Arbeitsvertrag im voraus auf einen Zeitraum von weniger als einer Woche beschränkt ist, nach Maßgabe der Vorschriften dieses Gesetzes gegen Krankheit zu versichern.

Reichs-Gesetzbl. 1883.   15

Ausgegeben zu Berlin den 21. Juni 1883.

Germany was one of the first countries in the world to set up a scheme of national insurance for the workforce. In 1883 a *Reichsgesetzblatt* (State regulation) was published (*left*), stating in the name of Wilhelm ('by God's mercy German Emperor, King of Prussia...') that all workers were to be insured against sickness. (*Opposite*) An imposing villa, in the Grunewald district of Berlin, which was used as an office to supply vouchers in settlement of invalidity and pension claims in the 1890s.

The advances in science and technology that revolutionised people's lives towards the end of the 19th century flared with especial brilliance in Germany. The electrical industry began in the 1860s, with AEG and Siemens establishing an early world lead. (*Above*) A glass-blowing workshop in the AEG factory in Berlin, c. 1890. The women workers are producing light bulbs for the new commercial and domestic markets. (*Opposite*) Potsdamer Platz, Berlin, in 1884. The street was the heart of the city and the centre of its night-life. It was also the first in Germany to be lit with electric light.

For those that had, life became better and better. There was more to see, more to do, more money to make, more places to go. Ernst Litfass capitalised on the new wealth by inventing the advertising column (*right*) on which promoters could place advertisements for goods, concerts, plays, sales. (*Opposite*) One of the many grand villas developed in all the major cities of Germany towards the *fin de siècle* – the Villa Wieck in Bismarckallee, Berlin. Traditional elements of German architecture and design were much in favour, though houses such as this would also have all the modern conveniences of life.

Great minds produced new philosophies, new novels, new thoughts on the meaning of life, new ways of dealing with other, more troubled minds. (*Below, left to right*) Theodor Fontane, poet and novelist; Hans Theodor Woldsden Storm, poet and writer of stories with an eerie descriptive power; and Richard Dehmel, a poet much influenced by Nietzsche.

(*Below, left to right*) Friedrich Nietzsche, the most powerful of German philosophers and author of *Also sprach Zarathustra*; Sigmund Freud, physician and pioneer of psychoanalysis; and Theodor Mommsen, among the greatest of German historians and winner of the Nobel Prize in 1902. (*Left*) The 17th-century border bridge at Berwick-on-Tweed, Northumberland. Theodor Fontane, the most important exponent of the German 'society novel', full of wit and humour, spent several years in England as a correspondent. He travelled to Scotland where he described beautifully the Border country around the River Tweed.

Orchesterskizze der Trauerklänge zu Siegfried's Tod.

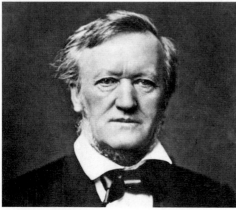

Richard Wagner (*left*) was born in Leipzig in 1813. He began composing operas in his mid-twenties, and had his first success with *Rienzi* in 1842. From then until his death in 1883, Wagner produced a series of music-dramas that have never been surpassed. (*Above, left*) The cover of a programme for the season at the Bayreuth Opera House in 1884. Wagner settled in Bayreuth in the 1870s, when Ludwig of Bavaria offered to build a theatre large enough to house Wagner's productions of his works. (*Above, right*) A page from Wagner's original manuscript of *Nibelungenlied* with the vocal line and accompaniment for the death of Siegfried.

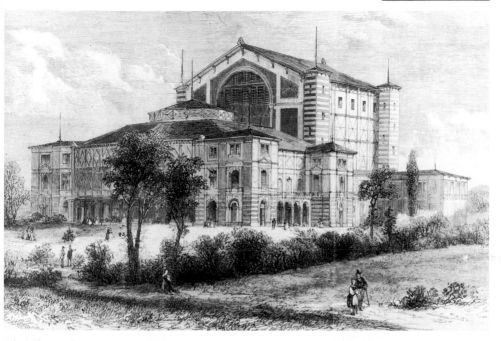

(*Above*) The opera house at Bayreuth, just before the official opening in August 1876 with a performance of *Der Ring des Nibelungen*. (*Right*) The baritone Anton von Rooy, who first filled the role of Siegfried in Wagner's *Ring*. (*Far right*) Zdenka Fassbender as Brunhilde in *Die Walküre*, c. 1900.

14
THE WILHELMINE EMPIRE
1890–1914

Most European nations look back on the days before the First World War as a time of long hot summers, innocence, pastoral peace and quiet, and gentle leisure. It is a false picture for all but the few who could afford the riches that were on offer. For wealthy Germans, there was much to enjoy in town and country – a ride in a new motor car, a trip to the country villa, a day by the sea, an evening in a fashionable restaurant. For the Rothschild family (*right*), there was little to beat a pleasant day on the beach, lounging in wicker chairs and watching the children build their sandcastles. Castles in the air were a different matter…

Introduction

Edward VII of Britain – not the most generous-natured of men – described his nephew Wilhelm II of Germany as 'the most brilliant failure in history'. Not surprisingly, Wilhelm loathed England, and had his English mother placed under house arrest the moment his father died.

The Kaiser had little time for laws or people who got in his way. When he came to the throne, he predicted a clash with Bismarck. 'I'll let the old boy potter along for another six months,' he told friends, 'then I'll rule myself.' Once Bismarck had been disposed of, Wilhelm's rule was brash and aggressive.

The empire he ruled was enormously rich, both culturally and economically, and life for the young state was full of incident and excitement. Marx, Freud and Einstein stood life on its head, shattering thoughts and principles that had been accepted for hundreds of years. Society came under the microscope of a new science – sociology – pioneered by Max Weber. Behrens,

Messel and Hoffman built a new set of rules for architecture. Thomas Mann set out on the road that was to lead to a Nobel Prize for Literature: a series of brilliant dramas ensured that Gerhart Hauptmann got there before him. Brahms and Mahler fashioned their last symphonies with tonal magnificence: Schönberg and Webern rewrote the musical scale. Expressionist writing and art received encouragement from two new magazines – *Aktion* and *Sturm*. Franz Marc painted *The Blue Rider* (which led to the founding of a group of Expressionist artists known as *Der blaue Reiter*). Marc's work subsequently joined Van Gogh's *Sunflowers* as one of the most reproduced paintings of all time.

In the material and increasingly military world, there was much to marvel at and applaud. Work began on the Berlin–Baghdad railway. The Kiel Canal was opened in 1895. Under the supervision of Grand Admiral Alfred von Tirpitz, the mighty battleships of the imperial navy came to rival, if not surpass, those of Britain. The railway network grew by 14 per cent per year. Steel and iron production increased tenfold.

Clothes had never been so elegant, houses so comfortable, café society so enticing. There were new fads and fashions to delight young and old – new dances, and new crazes such as roller-skating and ice-yachting. The Theater des Westens – a home for light opera – opened in Charlottenburg in 1896, and the first German cinema (the Bioskop in the Berlin Wintergarten) in 1895. Max and Emil Shladonowsky were just a few months ahead of the Lumière brothers in showing the world's first moving pictures. Max Reinhardt took over the direction of the acclaimed Deutsches Theater, and the New People's Theatre opened in Berlin in 1910.

And, to the delight of fathers everywhere, Märklin produced the first toy train sets.

In public, the Kaiser was rarely seen out of uniform. He spent much of his life with the army and his chiefs of staff. The threat of war was everpresent in the first years of the 20th century. (*Above*) The Kaiser Wilhelm II and von Moltke. (*Left*) The New Palace, Potsdam, 1912. (Left to right) The Kaiser, the Prince of Plessen, the Crown Prince, Eitel, Prince Adalbert, and August Wilhelm.

(*Above, left*) The celebrated cymbalist of the Kaiser's Imperial Guard. (*Above, right*) Herr Werner, chauffeur to Kaiser Wilhelm II, poses by the royal car. (*Right*) The Kaiser and his military advisers, c. 1910. Von Hindenburg is fourth from the right, Crown Prince Rupprecht is third from the left.

Aus großer Zei

v. Mackensen   v. Moltke   Kronprinz Wilhelm   v. François   v. Falkenhayn   v. Beseler   v. Bethmann-Hollweg
                              v. Preussen   Ludendorff   v. Einem
    v. Bülow   Kronprinz Rupprecht   Herzog Albrecht   v. Kluck   v. Emmich   v. Haeseler   v. Hindenburg   v. Heeringen
              v. Bayern   v. Württemberg   Kaiser Wilhelm II.   v. Tirpitz

The shipbuilding yards of north Germany were in full production. It was a golden age of ocean liners, and the imperial German navy was preparing to challenge the British fleet. (*Below, left*) Albert Ballin, the shipping magnate from Hamburg. He was a director of the Hamburg–America line and a naval adviser to the Kaiser. (*Above, left*) The Hamburg–America line *Vaterland* on her maiden voyage, 15 May 1914. (*Below, right*) The König class battleship *Kaiser Barbarossa* passing through the Kiel Canal in 1902.

(*Above*) The Eider Bridge over the river at Rendsburg. It was built entirely of iron, and was for a time the longest bridge in the world. Enthusiasm for such projects and for the programme of shipbuilding was immense. To industrialists the building of a new fleet offered large profits, to merchants the chance of increasing their trade, to patriots the long-awaited opportunity to wrest control of the seas from Britain, to workers and trade unionists the promise of plenty of work.

Control of the seas was to be matched by control of the skies. The maiden flight of the first Zeppelin took place on 2 July 1900. Development was rapid. (*Opposite, clockwise from top left*) Frau la Quiante prepares for the start of the Berlin Balloon Society race at Schmongandorff, 3 May 1908. Members of the *Reichstag* watch the Zeppelin LZ3 prepare to take off from Lake Constance, 1916. Count von Zeppelin's Mark II in 1909. A poster for the International Air Exhibition at Frankfurt in July 1909. (*Above*) A passenger-carrying Zeppelin operated by the German company Delag, the first scheduled airline company in the world, 1913.

(*Opposite, above*) Cars on the assembly line at the AEG factory in Berlin, 1900. (*Opposite, below left*) The British racing driver J. E. Hutton at the wheel of a Mercedes car on the Brooklands track, 6 July 1907. (*Opposite, below right*) The Mercedes stand at London's Olympia in 1911. Mercedes had already established a reputation second to none. (*Above, right*) The racing driver and automobile engineer Ferdinand Porsche drives an Austro-Daimler, 1910. (*Below, right*) A typical Berlin taxi of the years just before the First World War.

The bicycle played its own part in the transport revolution of the early 20th century. Cycle clubs arranged excursions into the countryside, rediscovering old villages and hamlets that had been neglected since the railways drove stagecoaches off the roads. (*Left*) A cycling club takes part in an historical pageant during the Berlin Gymnastics and Sports Week, 1910.

Two novel uses for the motor bike. (*Opposite, above*) A motor bike complete with fitted rear windshield serves as a pacemaker for the Berlin cyclist Alfred Koescher during a marathon race in Friedenau, c. 1900. (*Above*) A motor cyclist tows a skier across a barely adequate amount of snow, 12 January 1912. By this time the motor cycle also had far more important jobs to do in both military and civilian life.

Paul Ehrlich (*left*) was a German bacteriologist from Silesia. He was a pioneer in haematology and chemotherapy, and produced a treatment for syphilis, at that time a scourge among diseases. In 1908 Ehrlich was the joint winner of the Nobel Prize for Medicine. Max von Laue (*opposite, below left*) was a physicist and winner of the Nobel Prize in 1912. He was born near Koblenz, but spent most of his working life in Zurich, Berlin and Frankfurt. He was a far-sighted scientist, who predicted that X-rays could be diffracted by a crystal.

Perhaps the most famous German scientist of the early 20th century was Max Karl Ernst Planck (*above, right*). Planck studied at Munich and Berlin, and is best known as the formulator of the quantum theory, which revolutionised physics and paved the way for Einstein's theories of relativity. Friedrich Wilhelm Ostwald (*below, right*) invented a process for making nitric acid, a new theory of colour, and the dilution law named after him. He was awarded the Nobel Prize for Physics in 1909.

Haydn, Mozart, Beethoven, Weber, Mendelssohn, Schubert, Schumann, Wagner, Brahms, Liszt...the tradition of German musical excellence continued uninterrupted into the new century. (*Left, clockwise from top left*) Max Reger, composer, pianist, organist and teacher; Richard Strauss, chief conductor of the Berlin Court Opera and composer of many 20th-century masterworks; Arnold Schönberg, musical revolutionary and founder of the atonal school of composition; and Gustav Mahler, conductor and one of the last of the great symphonists.

(*Above, clockwise from top left*) Wilhelm Backhaus, one of the finest concert pianists of all time; Florizel von Reuter, a musical prodigy whose period of fame was brief but exciting; the pianist Germaine Schnitzel; and the composer and conductor Max Bruch.

The revolution in music, sponsored by Schönberg, was echoed by leading German artists at the same time. (*Left*) A poster of 1910 advertising the exhibition held by *Die Brücke* ('The Bridge') group in Dresden. The group was influenced by the Fauves, Gauguin, Van Gogh and Munch, and, despite its short life, had an immense influence on German art.

The other important group at this time was known as *Der blaue Reiter* school. The founder was Franz Marc (*above, right*) whose *Blue Horses* picture vies with Van Gogh's *Sunflowers* as being the most reproduced painting of all time. August Macke (*above, left*) was the co-founder of the group. Both Macke and Marc were killed in the First World War. (*Below, right*) A self-portrait by the painter and sculptor Käthe Kollwitz. Her work was strongly political, and she was later expelled by the Nazis from the Prussian Academy of Art.

Lovis Corinth (*left*) was an innovative painter who belonged to a generation older than the members of *Die Brücke* or *Der blaue Reiter*. His work later became a target for the Dadaists – in a Berlin night-club George Grosz mimed urinating on one of Corinth's canvases. Max Liebermann (*opposite, above left*), with Corinth and others, was one of the founders of the breakaway *Jugendstil* movement, the German equivalent of art nouveau. In May 1898 Liebermann and sixty-seven other artists formed the Berlin Secession, in protest at the teaching and practice of the Berlin Academy.

(*Far right*) The Hoch-
zeitsturm in Darmstadt, a
tower created by Joseph
Maria Olbrich as a
wedding gift for the
Grand Duke Ludwig and
Grand Duchess Eleonore
in 1905. (*Below, left*) The
Peter Behrens poster for
an AEG metal-thread
lamp, 1907. (*Below, right*)
The German painter Max
Slevogt, yet another
member of the Berlin
Secession group.

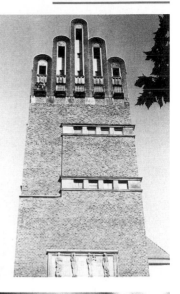

New riches were added to the wealth of German literature in the early 20th century. Karl May (*above, left*) was a writer of many westerns, and a student of Native American life (*above, right*). Georg Kaiser (*below, left*) was an Expressionist writer and dramatist, whose career lasted well into Weimar days. Gerhart Hauptmann (*left*) produced a succession of highly successful plays, including *Die Weber*, *Florian Gayer* and *Fuhrmann Herschel*. He won the Nobel Prize for Literature in 1912.

(Clockwise from top left) Franz Kafka, perhaps the best known of early 20th-century German writers. Kafka's novels *Der Prozess* (*The Trial*) and *Das Schloss* (*The Castle*) caught the mood of bewilderment and nightmare that gripped Germany after the First World War. Rainer Maria Rilke, the lyric poet whose work extended the range of expression and subtlety of the German language. Else Lasker-Schüler, author of *Der Malik* and *Mein blaues Klavier*. Thomas Mann, novelist and short-story writer. Many of his early short stories were published in *Simplicissimus*, the satirical magazine.

The Theater des Westens (*left*) opened in 1896 in Charlottenburg as the Berlin home for light opera, then much in vogue. In Weimar days, its cellar housed Trude Hesterberg's Wild Stage club. (*Below*) Tilla Durieux, actress on stage and screen (and in public life), and wife of Paul Cassirer. She was described by the writer and diarist Harry Kessler as 'a cold, hard woman'.

(*Right*) Tilla Durieux as Anitra in *Peer Gynt*. Cassirer was an art collector and publisher. Durieux's marriage to him was both exciting and depressing. She wrote: 'He became impossible. My very presence became intolerable to him...No one helped me. So I decided to leave...But a life without him was unimaginable, so I decided to kill myself...' In the end Durieux changed her mind, and it was Cassirer who killed himself.

Carl Hagenbeck (*left*) was a zoologist, animal trainer and circus director who established the Zoological Gardens in Hamburg in 1907. The distinction between animals as objects of study and wonder, and animals as objects of fun was not made in the early 20th century. (*Above*) Traditional circus fare – three riders on a single, but not blue, horse. (*Opposite, above*) The circus dentist makes a routine examination, c. 1900. (*Opposite, below*) Two walruses show no shame at the Hagenbeck Zoo.

The winter equivalent of a visit to the beach in the summer was an afternoon on the ice. Most German cities had ice rinks: those that did not certainly had ornamental lakes and ponds. In a country where the winter temperatures were often uncomfortably low, skating was a way of enjoying yourself and getting warm at the same time. Skates were relatively cheap, and there was no charge out in the open. The worst that could happen was multiple bruising – unlike swimming, where drowning was always a possibility.

(*Opposite*) A family takes to the ice, somewhere in Germany, c. 1900. Their neat jackets and embroidered skirts suggest that they are from a reasonably well-to-do home. Father is doubtless at home, reading the paper and smoking his pipe. Mother may be attending to household chores. Or, of course, it is just possible that they are both using the opportunity created by their children's absence for something more intimate. Chances were few and far between in the 1900s, when you had a large family. (*Above*) A lone skater on a frozen lake in a Berlin park.

In both Catholic and Protestant parts of Germany there was a long and healthy tradition of carnival. One of the biggest and best was held annually in Mainz, in February. (*Opposite, above*) Giant heads with heavily padlocked giant mouths in the Mainz Carnival of 1912. (*Above*) A float in the same carnival depicts John Bull of Britain attempting (unsuccessfully) to swallow the German navy. (*Opposite, below*) Children celebrate Ash Wednesday. The custom was to go from house to house in town or village demanding cakes.

In the last years before the First World War, the countryside had never looked so good. Standards of living had risen for agricultural workers, harvests were plentiful, the motor car and truck kept a respectful distance. (*Above*) German workers return from the fields with baskets full of asparagus. (*Left*) Three embarrassed peasant girls from Bavaria. War was soon to cut a swathe of sadness and loss through such village communities.

(*Right*) A young child helps to bring home the asparagus harvest. (*Far right*) Typical costumes worn by peasants from the Gutachtal valley in the Black Forest. (*Below, right*) A road winds through a steep-sided valley in Baden-Württemberg in the Black Forest. Although untouched by fighting, the inhabitants of such villages paid a heavy price for the military ambitions of others.

The greatest holiday and the greatest carnival of all was Christmas. It was a time of candles and presents, of Christmas trees and songs, of joy and thanks...and relief that the shortest day of the year was over. (*Opposite, above*) Pieces of wax which will be melted down in a Berlin factory to make Christmas candles for export throughout Europe. (*Opposite, below*) Racks of dolls for sale in a Berlin street market, 1910. (*Above*) Bringing home the tree for Christmas. Doubtless the cart had its uses at all other times of year as well.

15
RACING TO WAR
1900–1919

The nightmare landscape of the First World War – German infantry rest while retreating across the desolate countryside near the Chemin des Dames, northern France, May 1916. The area was to be fought over again and again. Shell holes filled with water in winter and wounded men drowned where they fell. Soldiers were ordered to advance with full pack across ground that was pitted and broken, where it was impossible to achieve more than a walking pace, in the face of murderous machine-gun fire. Commanders came and went. Von Moltke was succeeded by von Falkenhayn, von Falkenhayn by Hindenburg and Ludendorff. The ordinary soldier fought on and on, until he was killed or maimed.

Introduction

For over a hundred years, Germany had escaped the shame and horror of military defeat. When it came in 1918, it was traumatic and terrifying. Grete von Zieritz, a nineteen-year-old music student, described the atmosphere in Berlin: 'I went out of curiosity to the Royal Schloss and saw how the sailors tried to break down the iron doors. And the troops returning from the war – they were broken men. We watched them march with Hindenburg under the Brandenburg Gate and down Unter den Linden with tears in our eyes. There was a sense of doom in the air.'

Four years earlier, it had all been so different. 'You will be home before the leaves have fallen from the trees,' Wilhelm II told his troops as they left for the Front in August 1914. France reeled under an initial hammer-blow, and, until the

United States entered the war in 1917, Germany and Austria held their own against France, Britain, Russia and Italy.

The end came with a rush. The Bolshevik Revolution halted the war in the east and then travelled west to sow the seeds of mutiny in the German navy. Ludendorff's final offensive came within a whisker of success before losing impetus, grinding to a halt, and limping into reverse. Even so, when the guns were finally silenced in November 1918, German armies all stood on foreign soil.

That the war had lasted so long and that Germany had come so close to victory owed much to the ingenuity and determination that had placed the country in the forefront of science and technology, in peace as well as war.

Baron Manfred von Richthofen left the cavalry to command the 11th Pursuit Squadron of the German air force – his famous 'Flying Circus'. Ludendorff and Hindenburg were in a class apart from the commanders of the French, Russian and British armies. The German army was better armed, better trained, and better led.

Away from the war, Wilhelm Konrad von Röntgen stumbled across the X-ray, a source of light that penetrated flesh but not bone. The German car industry developed into the finest in Europe. Railways ran underground and on elevated tracks through Berlin.

There was much to fight for, and much to fight with. But the old empire and the old way of life sank for ever, like von Tirpitz's magnificent battle fleet in the cold depths of Scapa Flow.

It was the sunset of the imperial age. In Roman splendour, the heads of state in Austria, Germany, Russia and Britain wore their helmets, uniforms and medals, and strode along the carpets spread before them, but only George V of Britain (*left*, on horseback on the right with Wilhelm II) survived into the 1920s. (*Far left*) Kaiser Wilhelm II, in black plumed helmet, greets the Emperor Franz Josef, 26 March 1914. (*Below, left*) An earlier meeting between the Kaiser and Tsar Nicholas II, Bjoerkoe, 24 July 1905.

German territorial ambition in the early 20th century was directed towards Africa and the Middle East. There was much talk of Germany seeking 'a place in the sun'. After all, France and Britain had their colonial empires – why should Germany be excluded? German politicians began to woo the Ottoman Empire, and set about building the Berlin to Baghdad railway, which would pass through Constantinople (*above*), a city that had featured large in German history.

It was an ambitious project, and one that was likely to provoke protest from other powers – Britain in particular. (*Right*) August von Mackensen inspects a Turkish guard of honour at Sfirkedji Station in Constantinople, 24 March 1915. (*Below*) German soldiers on the Baghdad railway towards the end of the First World War.

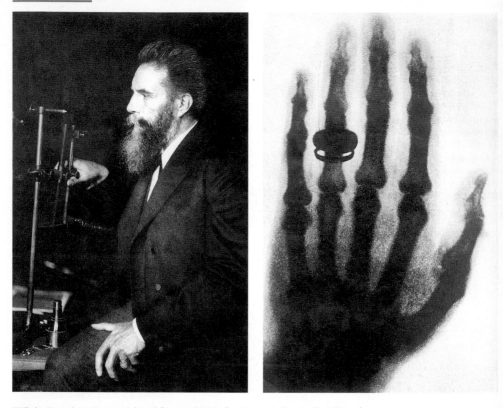

Wilhelm Konrad von Röntgen (*above, left*) was a physicist from Lennep in Prussia. On 1 November 1895, at Würzburg, he discovered electromagnetic rays that would pass through soft tissue, but could not penetrate bone or dense material. At first these rays were called 'Röntgen rays', but were soon renamed 'X-rays', simply because no one quite knew what they were. (*Above, right*) One of Röntgen's earliest X-ray pictures, showing his wife's hand, with the bones and her wedding ring clearly revealed.

The implications of the value of the X-ray were immediately apparent. Within a few days Röntgen's new apparatus had served to locate a nail swallowed by a young boy. Twenty years later, X-ray machines were in demand to locate bullets, shrapnel, splinters of shell by the hundreds of thousands, as the wounded were delivered to field and general hospitals behind the lines of war. (*Above*) German medical technicians with Röntgen apparatus, somewhere on the Western Front, 1916.

When it came, the war was greeted with general rejoicing. The spark that set the world ablaze was the assassination of the Archduke Franz Ferdinand and his wife Sophie in Sarajevo on 28 June 1914. (*Opposite, above right*) The royal couple moments before the assassination. (*Opposite, below*) The mobilisation order is read in a city square, August 1914. (*Opposite, above left*) German artillery leave for the front. (*Left*) Troops set off with smiles for a land of darkness.

(*Top*) Field Marshal Alfred von Schlieffen, whose plan dictated the early days of war. (*Above*) Helmuth von Moltke, director of German strategy at the outbreak of war. (*Left*) German infantry march through fields of flowers in the autumn of 1914.

The war effort at home had to match that of the troops in the trenches. The heart of German munitions production was the Krupp works at Essen (*left*). (*Below*) The interior of Krupp Cannon Workshop No. 5, shortly before the outbreak of war. Guns of every kind were produced here – for ships, planes, field artillery and siege weapons.

From workshop to battle-field. (*Right*) German soldiers loading shells into the chamber of a piece of heavy artillery, 1914. (*Below*) The largest cannon of the war: 'Big Bertha' in action, c. 1917. With a range of 122 kilometres, Bertha was able to bombard Paris for much of the later part of the war.

Never had war been waged on such a scale. Never had so many weapons been forged. Never had armies been amassed in such numbers. The war was fought in the skies, on the seas, but most of all on land. At first it was a war of movement. Austrian cavalry (*above*) moved east to do battle against Serbia and Russia. German cycle corps (*opposite, above*) were the new two-wheeled cavalry wing of the army. Even the old footslogger (*opposite, below*) was on the move – to Paris, to Berlin, to Moscow, to victory, to glory...to death...

The first major success for the German army was the Battle of Tannenberg, East Prussia, in August 1914. General Paul von Hindenburg (*above, left*, with Ludendorff on his right and Hoffmann on his left) defeated the Second Russian Army. (*Opposite, above and below*) German troops in action at the Battle of Tannenberg. Although the Germans lost 10,000 men, more than 100,000 Russians were killed. The statistics of war were instantly rewritten. (*Above, right*) A giant wooden statue of Hindenburg is unveiled, September 1914. Before the war was over, there were statues of Hindenburg in almost every town of any size in Germany.

As the combatants became bogged down on the Western Front, solutions were found to the problems of feeding and looking after troops in the squalor of the trenches. (*Left*) A travelling kitchen comes to rest in the mud of Flanders, 1916. (*Below*) One night's catch of rats in a single German trench, March 1916. Rats often carried disease.

Keeping hundreds of thousands of men adequately fed was a huge task for the commissariats of all the armies. Wherever possible, field ovens were installed to supply the men with bread (*right*). (*Below*) A portable altar and an open-air service meet the spiritual needs of a Catholic contingent of Uhlans in the early months of the war. Priests and chaplains often accompanied troops into battle.

The architect of the new German navy was Grand Admiral Alfred von Tirpitz (*left*). His first naval bill before the *Reichstag*, in 1898, had called for the building of two squadrons of battleships. Backed by a huge propaganda campaign, it proved to be a popular move, and a new naval bill in 1900 called for two more squadrons. When the war came, the German navy was strong enough to challenge the British, but both sides shied away from risking a trial of strength, and German warships (*above*) played little part in the conflict.

Death lurked below the surface of the sea. The weapons that ruled the waves turned out to be torpedoes and sub-marines. (*Above, right*) A German torpedo flotilla in Kiel harbour, 1914. (*Below, right*) A naval signaller sends a message to German troops landing at Osel in Russia, November 1917, the month of the Bolshevik Revolution. The following month, Russia signed an armistice with Germany.

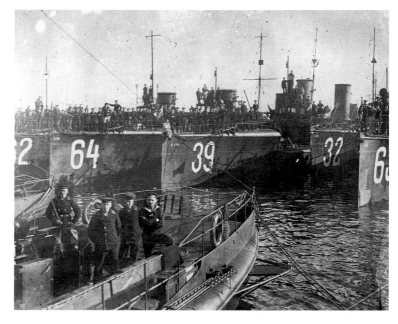

Leonardo da Vinci had dabbled with the idea, prototypes had been tried in the American Civil War, but not until the First World War did submarines become a real horror. They were used by all navies. (*Above, left*) British flags fly over a captured U-boat, 1917. (*Above, right*) Officers and men on board a German U-boat attempt to identify an approaching aircraft. (*Below, left*) A midget submarine docks alongside a U-boat, June 1917. (*Opposite, above*) The German U-boat base on Helgoland. (*Opposite, below*) A typical German U-boat. Such boats were destructively effective only at close range, but they were greatly feared by merchant ships.

Balloons had been used in the Franco-Prussian War of 1870–71. Their value was mainly as 'spotting' platforms, from which it was possible to watch troop movements or check the accuracy of artillery fire. (*Above, left*) German soldiers cast off the moorings of a giant air balloon. (*Below, left*) Two soldiers use pedal power to pump gas into a barrage balloon. (*Opposite*) A soldier leaps from his observation platform beneath a balloon that has been punctured by enemy action. Above him, a primitive parachute is about to open.

In a war involving millions of warriors, there were either too few or too many discernible heroes. But the people at home needed heroes, and the air forces of the protagonists provided them. Perhaps the greatest was Baron Manfred von Richthofen (*above, left*), known as the 'Red Baron'. Richthofen was in his early thirties when the war broke out. He became commandant of the 11th Pursuit Squadron, nicknamed 'Richthofen's Flying Circus'. With each enemy plane that he destroyed, his fame grew. At home, people demanded details of his lifestyle, his skills, his background. His dog Moritz (*above, right*) became the nation's pet.

(*Above*) Richthofen's mighty Flying Circus on parade, c. 1917. The machines are Fokker biplanes. In all, Richthofen destroyed eighty allied planes. Richthofen's career came to an end on 22 April 1918. He was killed when his plane was shot down over the battlefield of the Somme. Germany mourned the loss of one of its greatest war heroes. But the fighting went on.

Twentieth-century ingenuity had found new ways of killing, though the Wright brothers could at least have argued that they intended no harm when they invented powered flight. The same could not be said for the inventors of the submarine and the tank. (*Opposite*) A dog-fight between British SE-5s and German Fokker D7s, c. 1915. (*Above, right*) An airman boards a U-boat, June 1917. (*Below, right*) German drivers put captured British tanks through their paces. For a short while, tanks were a weapon of surprise for the British army.

Although allies, the Austrian and German armies were independent of each other. This occasionally led to confusion. After the Battle of Przemysl (100 kilometres east of Krakow) on the Russian front, German and Austrian armies found themselves marching in opposite directions to follow up their victory. (*Above*) Austro-Hungarian cavalry and German infantry pass each other in the streets of Przemysl, 3 June 1915.

The greatest concern at home was the shortage of food. Butter and cheese were in short supply. Butchers' shops offered crows, squirrels and even woodpeckers for sale. Coffee was almost un-obtainable. (*Above, left*) Inhabitants of Munich queue for their ration of potatoes, 1917. (*Below, left*) One of the hundreds of street soup kitchens to be found in German cities. This one is in Berlin.

(*Above*) German housewives queue for their ration books, 1918. (*Right*) The label on a packet of *Ersatz* sugar, costing 12 pfennig. 'But if you had the money you could go into the back room of almost any restaurant and get roast goose and strawberries and cream, and wash it all down with as much beer and champagne as you could hold. Meanwhile, ordinary people were making do on sparrow stew...,' wrote one Berliner.

When the war ended, the German fleet surrendered, and was taken to Scapa Flow in the Orkneys (to the north of Scotland), the principal British naval base. The ships stayed there until 21 June 1919. On that day, Admiral von Reuter gave the order that the ships should be scuttled. The entire fleet sank in the harbour. (*Above, left*) After scuttling their ship, the crew of the *Nürnberg* raise their hands to show that they are unarmed. They were, however, fired on by British troops. (*Below, left*) The *Hindenburg* in Scapa Flow.

(*Above, right*) Massive air locks rise above the hull of the *Kaiserin*, after the ship has been raised from the depths of Scapa Flow, 17 May 1936. As another war approached, the British needed scrap metal for a new generation of munitions. (*Below, right*) The remains of the German battleship *Friedrich der Grosse*, 16 September 1937. The ship was among those scuppered at Scapa Flow eighteen years earlier.

16
WEIMAR INTERLUDE
1919–1930

Within a month of the Armistice of November 1918, 2 million soldiers had returned to Germany. Chancellor Ebert hoped to use a considerable number of them to restore order in Berlin. It was not long, however, before a National Congress of Workers' and Soldiers' Councils had formed, based on Bolshevik principles. The Spartacist Revolution had begun in earnest, and the new government faced a massive challenge. (*Left*) 'All power to the Workers' and Soldiers' Soviets' – the Red Flag is carried through the streets of Berlin, December 1918.

Introduction

Bitter disillusionment gripped Germany. The Left offered a new future, but its champions were summarily dispatched. Karl Liebknecht and Rosa Luxemburg were horrifically murdered, and even the more moderate Walther Rathenau died in a hail of assassin's bullets. Gustav Stresemann succumbed to overwork in his heroic but vain attempt to find a political solution. Left and Right fought on the streets in ridiculous and impotent struggles to provide a revolutionary settlement. Communists and fledgling Nazis joined together in rent strikes, but the union did not last.

An Austrian ex-corporal took part in one unsuccessful *Putsch*, was sent to prison, and there dictated to his friend Rudolf Hess a book that was to become the bible of the Right. Never one to underestimate his importance, it was not long before Adolf Hitler was proudly pointing out what a rich prize he was for Germany: 'That is the miracle of our age...that you have found me among so many millions! And that I have found you, that is Germany's good fortune!'

Somehow the Weimar Republic managed to build on the creaking foundations of depression, devaluation and despair. From year to year, life went on. For the rich, there was the tasty diet of wine, women and song – the best of song coming from Fritzi Massary, Claire Waldoff and Rudolf Nelson. Hermann Frey and Paul Lincke produced the nonsense song of the age – a spoof of the American *Yes, We Have No Bananas* that was called *Mein Papagei frisst keine harten Eier* (*My Parrot Doesn't Eat Hard-boiled Eggs*). And the nonsense and frivolity, depravity and debauchery was all captured by the brush of George Grosz.

Nonsense made sense in the mad 1920s. The Dadaists were led by Hugo Ball, *Oberdada* Johannes Baader and Richard Huelsenbeck, who recited works of gibberish to the accompaniment of a big bass drum. The surreal Zirkus Busch opened in 1919. One act consisted of a man in top hat and eveningwear cooking an omelette while balancing on a tightrope. At his club on Weinbergsweg, the great clown Erich Carow rivalled Grock and Charlie Chaplin. Bigger and richer audiences gathered at the Wintergarten of the Central Hotel at Friedrichstrasse Station to hear the finest cabaret stars of the age. The most famous hotel in Germany was the Adlon in Berlin. It had its own well and generator, making it immune to strikes, street revolutions, the heat and the cold. It also had a manager who allowed some guests to stay free of charge.

On the night of 27–28 February 1933, Erich Carow was celebrating the twenty-fifth anniversary of his club. At 2 a.m. the *conferencier* for the evening, Werner Finck, joked: 'I see the Reichstag's been lit up for the occasion.' It was the funeral pyre of the Weimar Republic.

Sailors took the lead in the Spartacist Revolution. They took control of the centre of Berlin and persuaded government troops to join them. (*Above, left*) Sailors guard the Royal Palace in Berlin, December 1918. (*Below, left*) A machine-gun post on a Berlin house. (*Opposite, above*) The old order is swept aside – a bust of the Kaiser in a Cologne dustcart. (*Opposite, below left*) Revolutionary troops occupy the Royal Stables. (*Opposite, below right*) *Vorwärts* announces the Revolution, 9 November 1918.

2. Extrausgabe   Sonnabend, den 9. November 1918.

Vorwärts

Berliner Volksblatt.
Zentralorgan der sozialdemokratischen Partei Deutschlands.

Der Kaiser hat abgedankt!

Der Reichskanzler hat folgenden Erlaß herausgegeben:

Seine Majestät der Kaiser und König haben sich entschlossen, dem Throne zu entsagen.

Der Reichskanzler bleibt noch so lange im Amte, bis die mit der Abdankung Seiner Majestät, dem Thronverzichte Seiner Kaiserlichen und Königlichen Hoheit des Kronprinzen des Deutschen Reichs und von Preußen und der Einsetzung der Regentschaft verbundenen Fragen geregelt sind. Er beabsichtigt, dem Regenten die Ernennung des Abgeordneten Ebert zum Reichskanzler und die Vorlage eines Gesetzentwurfs wegen der Ausschreibung allgemeiner Wahlen für eine verfassunggebende deutsche Nationalversammlung vorzuschlagen, der es obliegen würde, die künftige Staatsform des deutschen Volkes, einschließlich der Volksteile, die ihren Eintritt in die Reichsgrenzen wünschen sollten, endgültig festzustellen.

Berlin, den 9. November 1918. **Der Reichskanzler.**
Prinz Max von Baden.

Es wird nicht geschossen!

Der Reichskanzler hat angeordnet, daß seitens des Militärs von der Waffe kein Gebrauch gemacht werde.

Parteigenossen! Arbeiter! Soldaten!

Soeben sind das Alexanderregiment und die vierten Jäger geschlossen zum Volke übergegangen. Der sozialdemokratische Reichstagsabgeordnete Wels u. a. haben zu den Truppen gesprochen. Offiziere haben sich den Soldaten angeschlossen.

Der sozialdemokratische Arbeiter- und Soldatenrat.

(*Above, left*) The new German Republic is proclaimed outside the Berlin Reichstag, 1 December 1918. (*Below, left*) Prince Maximilian von Baden, reluctant Chancellor of Germany at the end of the First World War. (*Below, right*) Philipp Scheidemann, the socialist who replaced Maximilian von Baden.

(*Above*) The initial Weimar government – Gustav Noske, who put down the Spartacist Revolution, is second from left, top row. (*Right*) Friedrich Ebert, social democrat and first President of the German Republic, addresses an assembly at Harm, 1 March 1923.

While much of Germany sought to return to normal, Berlin was torn apart by the Spartacist Revolution and attempted coup. (*Above, left*) Armed Spartacists commandeer a car in Berlin, 8 January 1919. 'Order and calm are necessary concomitants to the successful conclusion of the revolution. Citizens are requested to keep off the streets wherever possible…' (*Below, left*) Government soldiers and Spartacists battle for control of the Berlin streets.

(*Right*) Pamphlets seized from newspaper offices are burnt on the streets during the Spartacist rising. (*Below, left*) A mass demonstration during the days of struggle and violence early in 1919. (*Below, right*) Rosa Luxemburg, the Marxist revolutionary who was brutally murdered while in army custody on 15 January 1919.

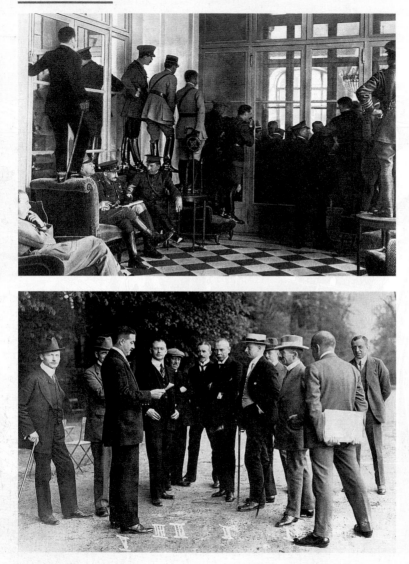

(*Above, left*) Henry Guttman's photograph of British and French officers standing on chairs to observe events in the Hall of Mirrors during the negotiations at Versailles, 28 June 1919. (*Below, left*) German delegates at the Versailles peace talks, 7 May 1919. The conditions imposed upon them were ludicrously punitive. Germany was ordered to pay the entire costs of the war.

When the terms of the Peace Treaty became known, there was widespread protest in Germany. (*Above, right*) Women demonstrate against the Peace of Versailles, 1919. As well as paying vast reparations, Germany was ordered to disband almost its entire armed forces. (*Below, right*) Under the terms of the peace, propellers from German fighter planes were reduced to kindling wood.

At no time could the Weimar Republic be said to have enjoyed a period of stability, but under the chancellorship of Gustav Stresemann relative calm prevailed. Stresemann sought to establish better relations with the rest of Europe – to the anger of the extreme left- and right-wing groups in Germany. (*Above, left*) Stresemann and his wife, c. 1929. (*Above, right*) Walter Rathenau, the German industrialist, founder of AEG, and Minister of Reconstruction in the Weimar Republic. He was assassinated in 1922.

Gustav Stresemann addresses the League of Nations
(*above*) on the occasion of Germany's admittance, 1926.
(*Right*) An extract from Stresemann's speech: 'The
felicitous future of the peoples rests on their goodwill in
respecting equal entitlement to freedom upon the
combined endeavours of their leaders to organise and
develop peace and international life…' Stresemann was
joint winner of the Nobel Peace Prize in 1926.

(*Left*) Leaflets flutter down on a Berlin street during the Kapp *Putsch* of March 1920. The French and British demanded the disbanding of some of the German *Freikorps* units. Colonel-General Hans von Seeckt refused. The right wing was on the verge of snatching power, but Wolfgang Kapp proved unequal to the task. (*Below*) Right-wing troops during the Munich beer-hall *Putsch* of 1923.

The years slipped by without any resolution between right and left. By 1927 both sides had armed followers on the streets. (*Above, right*) Members of the anti-Fascist Red Front. (*Below, left*) Yet another protest, this time by anti-war demonstrators and members of the Association of Friends of Religion and Peace Among Nations, 1927. (*Below, right*) The German Communist leader, Ernst Thälmann, gives a clenched fist salute.

For the hundreds of thousands of ex-soldiers, work was scarce in the 1920s. Many tried to eke out a living as street vendors, selling bootlaces, matches, toys, soap or trinkets (*left*). Some women were better off, for they managed to keep jobs that they held while the men were away fighting. (*Below, left*) A woman assembles a toy steam engine in a Nuremberg factory. (*Below, right*) One of the many German families who made their homes in old railway trucks in the 1920s.

(*Right*) Two young boys share a cigarette in Berlin. The breakdown in traditional family life caused grave concern. Children appeared lawless and undisciplined. Gangs of youths roamed the streets. Young girls drifted into prostitution, sometimes with their mothers acting as their 'madames', their fathers as their pimps. On the farms around Berlin, farm workers patrolled the fields with shotguns, to scare off those stealing the harvest.

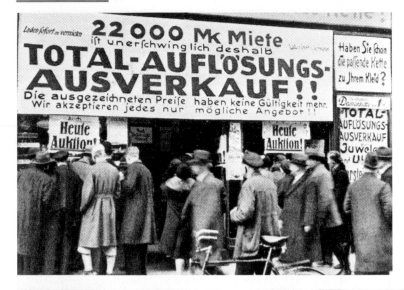

The German mark collapsed in 1923. (*Left*) A store paying 22,000 marks a month rent announces that it is closing. (*Below, left*) Foreign currency is exchanged on the street. (*Below, right*) Children play with worthless banknotes. (*Opposite, above and below*) Vouchers and banknotes from 1921 to 1923. The vouchers are valid for a limited period only.

The British and French stuck to the harsh terms of the Peace of Versailles for as long as possible, despite the impossibility of Germany being able to pay. (*Above, left*) A French soldier stands guard on a trainload of coke on the outskirts of Cologne, 1920. The fuel is intended for France, as part of the reparations repayment. (*Above, right*) A French official oversees the demolition of the Krupp factory at Essen during the French occupation of the Ruhr, 1923.

The stigma of having foreign troops on German soil so long after the end of the war created increasing bitterness, and helped pave the way for the rise of the Nazi party in the late 1920s and early 1930s. (*Right*) German children line up to collect food from French soldiers during the occupation of the Ruhr. (*Below*) French troops patrol the streets of Bochum, 1923.

As well as suffering occupation, the demolition of factories and workshops, the destruction of planes, and the payment of vast penalties, the German people were forced to hand over some of the jewels of German endeavour. (*Above*) The former Hamburg–America line *Bismarck* in South Boston Dock, England, undergoing a refit for the British-owned White Star line. The liner was one of several taken from Germany in the early 1920s.

(*Right*) The former Hamburg–America line *Imperator* (on the right), renamed *Berengaria* and now flying the Cunard flag, leaves Southampton Docks, May 1922. (*Above*) Awaiting a new life, and a new master – propellers on a German liner dwarf the port of Bremen in the background.

But it was still possible to get away from it all. Even while the Spartacist Revolution was taking place at the end of 1918, Berliners hurried from store to store, doing their Christmas shopping. Communists and fascists fought and shot at each other, but the clubs and bars were open, and there were pretty girls to be seen in the cabarets and theatres. (*Above, left*) Unicyclists on a Berlin street. (*Above, right*) Carla and Eleanor, the 'G Sisters', an internationally famous singing act. (*Opposite, clockwise from top left*) Gateway to heaven – a cabaret entrance, c. 1925; the twin daughters of the director of the Berlin Opera House; and those who preferred dancing to the revolution in the streets.

In the 1920s German film production equalled and many times surpassed the best of the rest of the world. There was talent in abundance, and technical equipment to match. Fritz Lang (*above, left*) was an outstanding director of such silent masterpieces as *The Testament of Dr Mabuse* (said to have been a warning against the ambitions of Hitler), *Niebelungen* and *Metropolis*. (*Above, right*) Set designers at work on the construction of a futuristic background for one of the scenes in *Metropolis*, 1925.

The leading production company was Universum Film Aktiengesellschaft, makers of *Metropolis*. It was an epic, a powerful futuristic study (set in the year 2000) of the individual fighting against the state. It took seventeen months to finish, cost 2 million marks, and used 35,000 extras. It was an art deco triumph. Two scenes from *Metropolis*. (*Above, right*) Gustav Fröhlich as Fredersen, the hero of the film. (*Below, right*) Rudolf Klein-Rogge straps poor Brigitte Helm into his fiendish mind-blowing machine.

(*Opposite*) The incomparable Marlene Dietrich, who made her name in the 1929 film *Der blaue Engel* (*The Blue Angel*). It was the film that brought her to the attention of Hollywood. (*Right, clockwise from top left*) Hertha Thiele, star of the acclaimed and discomfiting film *Mädchen in Uniform*; Elisabeth Bergner, the first film actress to play a lead in George Bernard Shaw's *St Joan* – it opened in Berlin before London; Brigitte Helm, victim and villain in *Metropolis*; and Lil Dagover, heroine and star of Erich Pommer's *The Cabinet of Dr Caligari*.

No other country had so many film directors of such vision and artistry. (*Opposite, above*) Walter Ruttman, abstract film maker and editor of *Berlin, Symphony of a Big City* in 1927. (*Opposite, below*) Film director Ernst Lubitsch and actor Emil Jannings. (*Above, left*) Marlene Dietrich and Josef von Sternberg, director of the sensational *Der blaue Engel*. (*Above, right*) The Austrian director, writer and actor Erich von Stroheim as Prince Nikki in the 1928 film *The Wedding March*. Like so many stars of the German film industry, von Stroheim later sailed for Hollywood.

As in film, so in ballet – German choreographers and dancers were among the foremost in the world during the 1920s. (*Opposite, above right*) Marie Wiegmann (Mary Wigman), dancer and choreographer, in 1925. She made her début in 1919 and the following year founded a dance school for 'expression dance'. (*Above*) Members of her dance school in the open air, 1925. Wiegmann was one of the most influential teachers of dance, and is reckoned to have been the creator of the dramatic-expressive solo dance. She retired from her school in 1967.

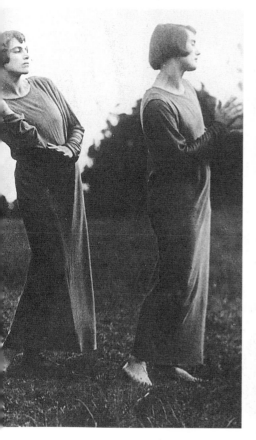

(*Right*) The German dancer Valeska Gert poses on a hamper
in a 1926 ballet. Gert shocked audiences in France with her style
of dance, which owed much to that of Isadora Duncan. Her
dances were like little plays, stories or biographies, exploring
episodes in the lives of the characters she created. She opened her
own cabaret in Berlin – the Kohlkopp – and later ran a bar in
New York.

(*Above, left*) Max Reinhardt, manager of the Deutsches Theater, rehearses Lady Diana Cooper in the 1925 production of *The Miracle*. (*Above, right*) Felix Ernst Witowski, also known as 'Maximilian Harden' and 'Friend of Bismarck', theatre and literary critic, and adviser to Max Reinhardt. (*Below, left*) An impromptu crowd gathers to watch a street performance of Wilhelm Busch's travelling theatre, Berlin 1929.

(*Above, left*) Maria Orska became famous for her roles in the plays of Oscar Wilde and Franz Wedekind. She killed herself in 1930. (*Above, right*) Fritz Kortner in a film version of the musical *Chu Chin Chow*. Orska left her banker husband to elope with Kortner. (*Right*) The singer and actor Fritzi Massary, 'Queen of the Operetta'. She and her husband Max Pallenberg, with Erich Maria Remarque, Kortner and the actor Albert Bassermann, formed a clique that frequently met at the Eden Bar.

On 31 August 1928 *The Threepenny Opera* (*above*) opened at the Theater am Schiffbauerdamm in Berlin, with words by Berthold Brecht and music by Kurt Weill (*left*). 'Up until the second scene it looked as if we had a failure on our hands. Then came the *Cannon Song*. There was an unbelievable storm from the auditorium. The public roared. From that moment we couldn't go wrong…' (Lotte Lenya). (*Opposite*) Another Brecht masterpiece – *Mother Courage and her Children*. Brecht (centre, seated) rehearses members of the Berliner Ensemble, including Helene Weigel (left), Angelika Hurwitz and Erwin Geschounik.

The Café Adler in Nollendorfplatz, Berlin, was the meeting-place for many writers and critics, among them Alfred Döblin (*below, left*). Döblin's greatest work was the rambling, brilliant novel of the human condition in a disintegrating social order, *Berlin Alexanderplatz*, published in 1929. (*Left*) Berlin in the late 1920s. (*Below, right*) Ernst Toller, a writer who was imprisoned for his political views, and author of *Masse Mensch*, *Die Maschinenstürmer* and the autobiographical *Eine Jugend in Deutschland*.

(*Right*) The opening of the Dada Fair, Berlin, 5 July 1920 – (from left to right) Raoul Hausmann, Otto Burchard, Baader, Wieland and Margarete Herzfelde, George Grosz, John Heartfield; (seated) Hannah Höch, Otto Schmalhausen. (*Below, left*) Kurt Tucholsky, writer and critic, and contributor to the Berlin cabaret scene. (*Below, right*) Lion Feuchtwanger, author of *Jud Süss*.

(*Above*) The interior of the Bauhaus School in Dessau in 1930. 'The goal of all creative activity,' wrote Gropius in a manifesto of 1919, 'is building…' Teachers there included Klee, Kandinsky, Mondrian, Marcel Breuer, Albers and Schlemmer. (*Right*) The Vassily chair, designed by Marcel Breuer in 1925. It was first produced by Standard Furniture of Berlin in 1926 and was still in production in the 1990s.

It had been a success in war. In peace it became a wonder and a delight. (*Left*) The skeleton of the giant *Graf Zeppelin LZ127* under construction, September 1928; and (*opposite, above right*) flying over the Brandenburg Gate later the same year. It was designed by Count Ferdinand von Zeppelin (*opposite, above left*). The standard of luxury offered by the *Graf Zeppelin* was extraordinary. (*Opposite, below left*) The first-class lounge of the airship. (*Opposite, below right*) The kitchen area. Few German homes could match such modern design and equipment.

Tempelhof Airport, Berlin (*left*), was opened in 1923, and was for several years the most advanced airport in the world. Three years later, Junkers Luftverkehr AG and Aero-Lloyd merged to form Deutsche Luft-Hansa, with flights to fifteen European cities. (*Below*) A Junkers D-2000 on the tarmac at Tempelhof in 1930. It was one of the largest planes in the world.

(*Right*) A fifteen-seater Luft-Hansa airliner, March 1928. The company's main office was in Mauerstrasse, and offered a car service to the airport. (*Below*) Intrepid passengers caught between the perils of air and sea after a demonstration of the Rohrbach and Dornier flying-boat at Lake Wannsee, near Berlin, c. 1925.

17
NEW ORDER
1930–1939

The pace of the march to war quickens. (*Right*) German troops pass through the gates of Hradschin Castle, Prague, during the occupation of Czechoslovakia, 1939. It was the year when Jews were forbidden to practise as dentists or chemists, when the *Bismarck* was launched, when Gandhi called on the world to disarm, and when France and Britain agreed to support Poland if Hitler threatened to invade. It was the year in which only the most optimistic could hope that Europe was not about to go up in flames.

Introduction

Some have been tempted to view the history of Germany in the 1930s as some Wagnerian drama in which the forces of evil enslaved an entire population, to follow the cruellest code the world has ever known. It is not difficult to find evidence of the evil – in the midnight arrests of Jews and Communists, trades unionists and liberals; in *Kristallnacht*, when the windows of Jewish shops were shattered; in the burning of books deemed decadent by a regime that was frightened of the ideas expressed by its own people; in badges of shame that were worn with arrogance; in parades and torchlit processions designed to terrify rather than impress.

But despite Nazi rule from 1933 onwards, there were times and places when hardly a swastika was to be seen. The Führer may have hijacked the 1936 Olympics for ends that should have provoked the Olympic Committee to greater protest, but Berlin remained the setting for feats of strength and skill rarely rivalled since, and Leni Riefenstahl's film *Olympia* is still one of the triumphs of cinema.

Indeed, the whole German film industry was the finest in Europe, though many of its top actors and directors would be gone before the decade was over. Peter Lorre, Conrad Veidt, Emil Jannings and Marlene Dietrich all left for the United States. Max Ophüls, Billy Wilder and Fritz Lang followed. German music lost the singer Richard Tauber and two of the finest conductors of the 20th century – Otto Klemperer and Bruno Walter. The writer Erich Kästner saw his own books burnt in the fires of 10 May 1933 and recalled Heine's line: 'Where they burn books, sooner or later they will also burn people.'

On the new Autobahns of the Reich and the new Avus racing circuit, German cars were fast and sleek. Fritz von Opel emerged as the winner of the first meeting held at Avus in September 1921. Alfred Neubauer, racing manager of Mercedes, was perhaps the greatest team leader of all time. In 1939 Porsche introduced the humble (later 'classic') Volkswagen. Streamlined German trains, diesel powered, slipped along the rails that joined the country's major towns and cities. The *Hindenburg* airship purred overhead, until the terrifying explosion by the mooring mast at Lakehurst, New Jersey, on 6 May 1937.

And yet, upstage but moving inexorably towards the footlights, the army of the Nazis was on the march. In 1936 came the re-militarisation of the Rhineland, in 1938 the *Anschluss* with Austria and the occupation of the Sudetenland. There was only one more border to cross before Europe went to war.

When this photograph (*above*) was taken in 1930, President Paul von Hindenburg (standing) was eighty-two. His triumphs were all in the past. The present offered difficulties, the future promised disasters. Hindenburg had already been President of Germany for five years. He had a considerable sense of duty towards his country, but events were rushing ahead of him. He was simply no match for the aspiring and ruthless leader of the *Nationalsozialistsche Deutsche Arbeiterpartei*. The man in the top hat, behind Hindenburg, is Konrad Adenauer. His day was yet to come.

(*Above*) President Hindenburg shakes hands with his new Chancellor, Adolf Hitler, 1934. They had first met on 10 October 1931, when they were introduced to each other by General Kurt von Schleicher, a master of intrigue. They were not impressed. Hitler regarded Hindenburg as a dinosaur, a man totally out of touch with the needs and wants of Germany – as he saw them. Hindenburg looked down on Hitler as an upstart 'Bohemian corporal'. It was not a happy meeting, and the working relationship did not last.

It did not take long for the Nazis to make their presence felt, once they had come to power. The Locarno Pact of 1925 had established the demilitarisation of the Rhineland, but Hitler ordered its re-occupation and German troops entered in March 1936 (*left*) with swastikas flying.

By the mid-1930s the swastika was to be seen all over Germany. (*Right*) A woman offers a swastika to a passing motorist. It was most prominently to be seen beneath the eagles that surmounted columns along the length of Unter den Linden in Berlin, where the beautiful trees had all been felled to make way for this display of Nazi triumph (*opposite, above*).

'In the fight against decadence and moral corruption! In the name of breeding and rectitude in State and Family! I consign to the flames the writings of Heinrich Mann, Ernst Glaeser and Erich Kästner!' Kästner watched his own books burn (*above, left*) as he listened to the rantings of Goebbels, 10 May 1933. *Kristallnacht* was later. The windows of Jewish shops were smashed throughout Berlin and other German cities on the night of 9 November 1938. (*Below, left*) Friedrichstrasse on the morning after *Kristallnacht*.

The initial persecution of the Jews by the Nazis took many forms. They were compelled to wear a yellow star on their clothes (*above, left*); they had to add 'Israel' or 'Sara' to their names; their newspapers were banned...and there were the concentration camps. (*Above, right*) Anti-Jewish posters in the windows of Jewish shops. The English translation was for the benefit of foreign journalists.

...or was it Joy through Strength? The vogue for physical fitness in the 1930s was not confined to Germany, but few countries embraced it with such vigour. (*Above*) Intrepid members of the Hitler Youth Movement climb a fallen tree in a Berlin park, 26 June 1936. It was the sort of thing young boys were doing all over the world on a summer afternoon. (*Left*) This, on the other hand, was a little out of the ordinary...

(*Above*) The spirit of Isadora Duncan lived on in Nazi Germany. Healthy (and essentially attractive) nudism was applauded and praised in Nazi-sponsored art and sport. (*Right*) The original British caption to this photograph read: 'Judging by this picture, Germany too has been experiencing fine and warm weather. Here are pretty girl members of one of Germany's many health movements showing their paces near Berlin.' It was less than a month since the *Anschluss*.

Whatever its aims, the Hitler Youth movement offered challenging and healthy activities for many children starved of such occupations during the 1920s. (*Above*) Young members of the *Pimpfe* organisation at their camp at Nowawes, near Potsdam, 13 October 1934. (*Left*) Young girls line the streets to cheer the Führer.

(*Above, right*) An early photograph of members of the Hitler Youth setting out on a hike, Munich, 1928. (*Below, right*) Boys and girls give the Nazi salute, October 1938. From 1939 onwards, membership of the Hitler Youth or the *Bund Deutscher Mädel* was compulsory for girls between ten and eighteen years of age. The fun and games were over. Young people were trained for war, and as spies against their own parents.

Robert Bosch (*left*) was a highly successful industrialist and an extraordinary man. He was the founder of a 'workshop for fine mechanics and electro techniques' in Stuttgart in 1896. The factory prospered and the company became public in 1916. Bosch was condemned by rivals for his supposedly 'red' or socialist views. He introduced an eight-hour working day for his employees in 1906 – an almost unheard of practice at that time.

(*Above*) The seventy-year-old Robert Bosch stands proudly in front of his company's stand at the Berlin Automobile Exhibition of 1931. Bosch had produced the first lamps for motor cars, back in the days of Daimler and Benz, and was still the leading company in this area. Suddenly and shockingly, the world around him changed. Bosch lived on till 12 March 1942, when he died in Stuttgart. He was spared the worst; that was yet to come.

The new stadium (*left*) designed by Werner March for the Olympic Games of 1936 was only one of a series of public works aimed at reducing unemployment. Like the *Autobahns*, the Air Ministry building, the Nuremberg Stadium and the new Chancellery, the Olympic complex did little to improve the life of ordinary people. It took all Goebbels' art of persuasion to convince Hitler that the Olympic Games should go ahead, for the Führer was convinced that the Games were 'a piece of theatre inspired by Jews'. Once convinced, however, Hitler was determined that the organisation of the Games should be of the finest, and that they should be remembered as 'the greatest festival of all time'.

(*Above, left*) Gustav Schäfer, winner of a gold medal for the single sculls rowing event at the Berlin Olympics. (*Above, right*) Hans Wolke set a new Olympic record with a throw of 16.2 metres in the shot put. (*Below, left*) German swimmers Erwin Sietas (centre) and P. Schwarz (right), salute on the winners' podium. (*Below, right*) A group of timekeepers perch on their ladder seat at the Berlin Olympics, August 1936. Each man has a different competitor to time. The closer the finish, the more difficult their work.

Leni Riefenstahl (*opposite*) was born in 1902 and was a ballet dancer before taking up a career as a film-maker. She became a brilliantly innovative cinematographer, using lighting and editing methods, as well as camera angles, which were way ahead of her contemporaries. (*Above, left*) Leni Riefenstahl as a film star in the Universal production *SOS Iceberg*. (*Below, left*) Riefenstahl plans a shot for her documentary study of the 1936 Berlin Olympic Games, *Olympia*.

59

The rapid annexation of other lands in central Europe by Nazi Germany was given a mixed reception by the inhabitants. There were those in the Sudetenland (*opposite, above*) who greeted the German troops as liberating heroes. In Austria, vast crowds turned out in Salzburg, waving swastikas in celebration of the *Anschluss* (*opposite, below right*), or to hear Heinrich Himmler speaking from the town hall in Linz (*above*), May 1938. Others, however, were less welcoming. Citizens of Prague maintained a sullen silence when the Wehrmacht entered their city in 1939. A few even spat on the soldiers (*opposite, below left*).

There were some who left as soon as the persecution began. There were others who settled their affairs and slipped away as inconspicuously as possible. And there were many who stayed on, hoping that things would change – until it became terrifyingly obvious that any change would be for the worse. (*Opposite, above and below*) Jewish refugees from Germany on the Hamburg–America liner *St Louis* arrive at Antwerp Docks, 17 June 1939. There, following a failed journey to refuge in Cuba, they would be safe – for a few months. (*Above, right*) Czech refugees from the Sudetenland settle for the night in a schoolhouse in Steti, near Malnic, 6 October 1938. (*Below, left and right*) The first batch of unaccompanied Jewish refugee children arrive in Harwich, England, 2 December 1938.

Though freedom of expression was in terminal decline, German writers continued to produce great works in the 1930s. Joseph Roth (*above, left*) was a regular contributor to the *Frankfurter Zeitung*, and the author of *Radetzkymarsch* and *Die Kapuzinergruft*. Heinrich Mann (*above, right*), elder brother of Thomas Mann, was a socially committed writer, critical of traditions of authoritarianism. Franz Werfel (*below, left*) achieved world fame with his novel *Die vierzig Tage des Musa Dagh*. The lyric poet Stefan George (*below, right*) refused the honours offered him by the Nazis and went into exile.

Erich Maria Remarque (*above, right*, with Carl Laemmle) wrote the definitive novel of the First World War – *All Quiet on the Western Front*. His books were banned by the Nazis, and, like Mann and Roth, Remarque went to the United States. The poet, essayist and dramatist Stefan Zweig (*below, left*) departed for exile in England in 1934. The writer Anna Seghers (*below, right*) was also forced to flee from the Nazis. She is seen here receiving the International Stalin Prize for 'The Promotion of Peace among Nations'.

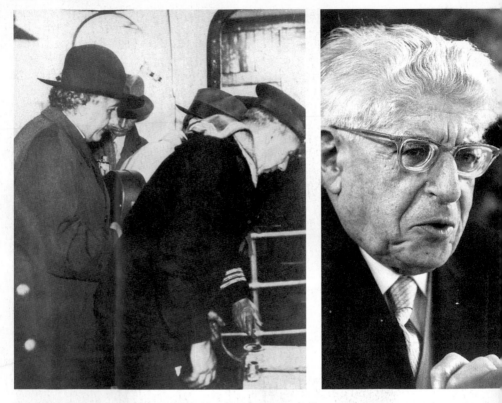

Writers, doctors, scientists, composers, musicians...the greatest minds in Germany haemorrhaged away.
(*Above, left*) Albert Einstein arrives in New York, 1933. (*Above, right*) The philosopher Ernst Bloch, who
also left Germany in 1933 for Switzerland and the USA. (*Opposite, above left*) The brilliant film actor
Peter Lorre, who starred in many German silent and early sound films before emigrating to America in
1935. (*Opposite, above right*) Conrad Veidt as Rasputin in a film he made for MGM after leaving
Germany. (*Opposite, below*) The cast of the Free German Theatre prepare for a performance in London,
21 August 1943. They were just one of several theatrical companies who fled from Nazi rule.

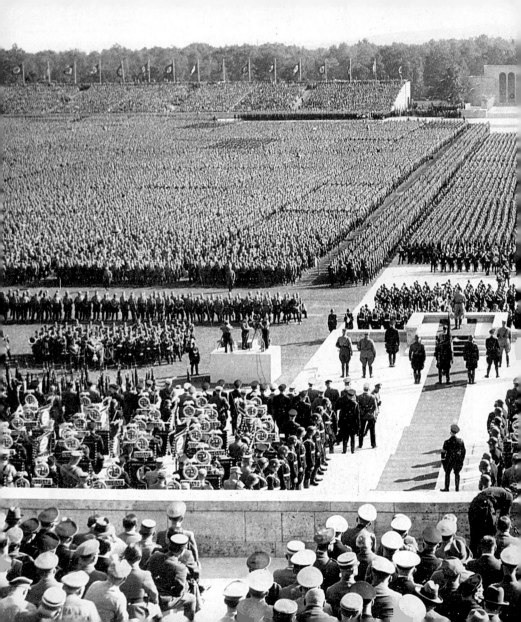

It was part of Hitler's Machiavellian cunning that he knew how to manipulate the German people. He knew the appeal of pageantry and ceremonial, the power of a torchlight procession, the comfort a nation can derive from a display of mass strength. Nowhere was such knowledge put to better use than in the mighty Nuremberg rallies. This was theatre on a terrifying scale. For a nation that had been in turmoil, confusion and international disgrace less than twenty years earlier, it was irresistibly seductive. (*Left*) The German Army on parade in the Nuremberg Stadium, September 1936.

Hitler's chief lieutenants were men who had joined the Nazi Party back in the early days: Goering and Himmler in 1922, Goebbels shortly after. (*Opposite*) Hitler and Goering exchange pleasantries during the Nuremberg Congress, 12 September 1938. (*Above, right*) Hitler and Joachim von Ribbentrop survey Germany's future through binoculars, 1939. (*Below, left*) Joseph Goebbels hurries to attend a session in the Reichstag, 3 December 1930. (*Below, right*) Professor Albert Speer shows his plans for a new Berlin to Adolf Hitler, 7 February 1938.

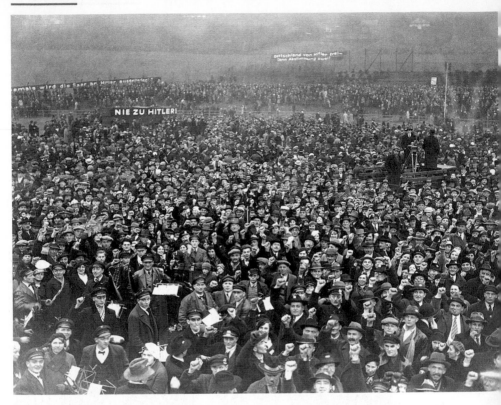

'One developed a kind of self-protection by screening oneself off from events,' wrote the actor Bernhard Minetti. 'That was probably the beginning of that suppression of feelings which would absorb the entire nation later on. From early on I avoided expressing any political opinion...' But there were many who worked and struggled and fought against the Nazis. (*Above*) An anti-Nazi and anti-Hitler meeting in Saarbrücken, 7 January 1935, during the plebiscite to determine the territory's future status. Many in the crowd are giving the clenched fist salute.

(*Right*) Pastor Martin Niemöller, a U-boat commander in the First World War, and later a priest and opponent of Hitler. He was sent to a concentration camp in 1938, but survived. 'In Germany,' he wrote, 'the Nazis came for the Communists and I didn't speak up because I was not a Communist. Then they came for the Jews and I didn't speak up because I was not a Jew...Then they came for the Catholics and I was a Protestant so I didn't speak up. Then they came for me...By that time there was no one to speak up for anyone.'

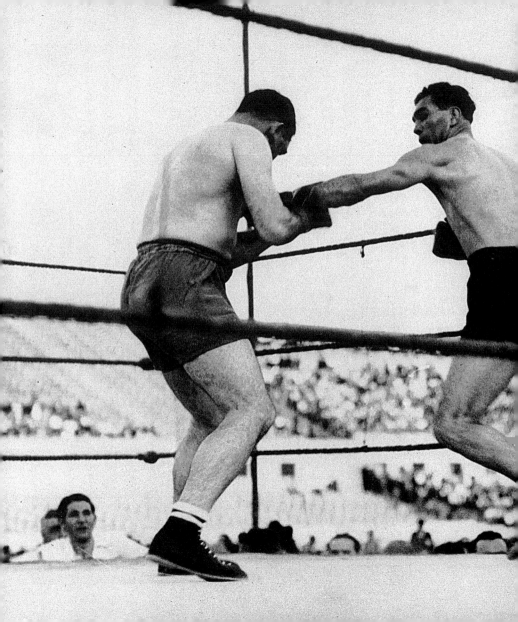

The boxer Max Schmeling (*left*) was World Light-Heavyweight Champion from 1927 to 1928, and World Heavyweight Champion from 1930 to 1932. He won the Heavyweight Championship on 13 June 1930 when he defeated Jack Sharkey in Yankee Stadium, New York, in front of 80,000 fans. He married the actress Anny Ondra, and retired to become a successful businessman. 'He was charming and shrewd. He invested his money from boxing wisely, and although he stayed on under the Third Reich, he did a lot to help those who were persecuted...' – Alfred Fischer.

One of the biggest programmes of public works in the 1930s was the construction of a network of *Autobahns* linking the major cities of Germany. (*Opposite, above*) Workers building the *Autobahn* linking Munich and Salzburg, March 1934. (*Opposite, below left*) The *Autobahn* linking Frankfurt and Mannheim in the 1930s. (*Opposite, below right*) Ferdinand Porsche, mechanic and inventor, and the man responsible for the Volkswagen 'Beetle', c. 1936. (*Right*) Hitler opens the factory where the 'People's Car' will go into mass production, 27 May 1938. It is still being produced.

18
WAR AND
RECONSTRUCTION
1939–1950

By the end of the war many German cities were in ruins. Those that had not become battlegrounds had been heavily bombed. Berlin was one of the worst affected, and was also the focus of Allied occupation. The task of restoring services and re-establishing a working administration was taken up by the occupying powers. The task of clearing the rubble fell to the citizens themselves. It was a way of earning enough food to survive the present, and of rebuilding the future. (*Right*) *Trümmerfrauen* – gangs of women who cleared the streets and bomb sites – at work in Berlin, July 1945.

Introduction

Seldom can a nation have experienced such an abrupt fall. In 1942 the empire of the Third Reich stretched from the Atlantic to the borders of Asia, from the icy wastes of Lapland to the deserts of North Africa. German troops once again occupied Paris. The German army appeared invincible, rolling back the Russians as it had brushed aside the British and the French.

Three years later Germany was broken, shattered and divided. Its erstwhile leaders were on trial, presented to the world as monsters of unspeakable depravity, and its population condemned by many as guilty by association. It was Berlin's turn to be occupied – by a four-power force of French, American, Russian and British military police who took turns to track down black marketeers and to shepherd displaced persons back to where it was thought they belonged. Groups of women known as

Trümmerfrauen crawled over the piles of debris in war-torn towns, doing what they could with their bare hands to remove the rubble left by bombing raids. Rats scuttled through the buildings that were still standing. Barter replaced money as the currency with which to buy and sell goods.

In what had once been the parks exuding civic pride, starving inhabitants raised vegetables in the summer and stripped the trees and benches of kindling in the bitter winters of the late 1940s. Refugees trickled back to the homeland – a pitiful few of them veterans of Operation Barbarossa, others who had survived the labour or concentration camps set up by their former rulers. Some families experienced the shock and joy of being reunited. Others were left to wonder what had happened to fathers, mothers, sons and daughters.

Somehow the people and the two Germanys lived on. East Germany became the protégé of the Soviet Union; West Germany the foster-child of the West. In the nick of time George Marshall of the USA formulated a plan to supply and feed people and regenerate industry. When modern ideologies clashed and the Soviet Union denied overland access to beleaguered West Berlin, modern technology came to the rescue. At its peak, the Berlin airlift delivered 7,000 tons of food and fuel in a single day.

And then the fog of deprivation and destruction, hardship and suffering began to clear. In 1948 a new currency – the Deutsche Mark – was introduced, and each citizen was given a grant of 40DM – little enough, perhaps, but a new beginning. The following year West Germany joined the Organisation for European Economic Development. Politically, economically and spiritually, West Germany at least was about to be reborn.

On 1 September 1939, planes of the Luftwaffe and troops on the ground began the invasion of Poland. The Polish army was heavily outnumbered and poorly equipped. Squadrons of cavalry were no match for divisions of tanks. (*Above*) The Wehrmacht advances along a Polish country road in the early days of the war. (*Opposite, above*) Prelude to the war – members of the Hitler Youth march over the Mottlau Bridge in the free city of Danzig, 11 May 1939. (*Opposite, below*) German soldiers dismantle the barrier between Poland and Germany, September 1939.

The initial strategy was to deliver knock-out blows to Poland and France, delay or avoid conflict with the Soviet Union, and make peace with Britain at the earliest opportunity. (*Above, left*) Hitler and Goering plan their tactics for the war in the west, 1940. There were other nations to be brushed aside. (*Below, left*) German paratroopers advance during the invasion of Crete, May 1941. The bodies on the right are those of British soldiers.

One of the countries to suffer early invasion was Norway. (*Above, left*) German planes bomb the Norwegian port of Narvik, 1940. The military importance of Narvik was that it remained an ice-free port in winter. By late 1941, however, hopes of a rapid and successful end to the war had faded. Britain was still fighting, and there were signs that opinion in the United States was increasingly turning against Germany. (*Above, right*) German army cyclists patrol a stretch of the Atlantic Wall defences, 1943. Eventually, the very size of German gains was to prove impossible to protect.

The fatal move came in June 1941, when Hitler ordered the invasion of the Soviet Union. At first the German advance was spectacular, with armies driving towards Stalingrad and Moscow. But Russian resistance was heroic...and then winter set in. (*Above*) German soldiers retreat from the Ukraine during a snowstorm, 10 February 1943. (*Left*) A lone soldier keeps look-out for the Red Army on a gun emplacement near Orel.

The terrible retreat from Moscow. Waist deep in mud, German soldiers haul a staff car through the bleak Russian landscape (*above*). The losses and the suffering were horrific. Hundreds of thousands of men died. Hundreds of thousands more were taken prisoner. (*Right*) Members of the Wehrmacht's crack Police Division manhandle their field guns into position on the Russian front.

One of the greatest successes for German armed forces was achieved by the Afrika Korps under Field Marshal Erwin Rommel. In a series of brilliant moves, Rommel and his men overran North Africa, from east to west. (*Above*) Members of the Afrika Korps on patrol in Libya. (*Left*) A camouflaged Messerschmitt fighter flies over the African desert, 1942.

(*Above*) Cultures collide. Desert donkey – two Libyan boys are passed by an Afrika Korps tank near Tripoli, 1 December 1942. Desert Fox – Field Marshal Rommel (*right*) takes leave of Benghazi, 5 December 1942. The U-boat waiting to take him home is in the background.

In June 1944 a group of Wehrmacht officers made a brave but unsuccessful attempt to assassinate the Führer. They placed a bomb in Hitler's army headquarters. The building was wrecked (*above, left*). Hitler survived. The conspirators were executed: (*below, left*) Dr Carl Friedrich Goerdeler, *Bürgermeister* of Leipzig; Fritz, Graf von der Schulenburg (*opposite, above*, with his family); Claus, Graf von Stauffenberg (*opposite, below left*, with his children); and Helmuth James, Graf von Moltke (*opposite, below right*).

From the early 1930s there had always been many prepared to resist the Nazis. By 1939, however, most of Hitler's opponents had been crushed or driven underground. The outbreak of war allowed the Nazis to brand all opposition as treasonable. Bravest of those who resisted the Nazis from within the heart of Germany were members of the White Rose resistance group. Hans Scholl (*above, left*) and Christoph Probst (*above, right*) were students who called on their comrades to fight Nazi oppression. Hans's sister Sophie Scholl (*opposite*, arms raised) joined them, distributing anti-Nazi leaflets. All three were arrested and executed.

Though later outnumbered and over-stretched for resources, the Luftwaffe was superbly equipped in the Second World War. (*Left*) Willy Messerschmitt, designer and production head of the biggest German aircraft firm. (*Above*) A Messerschmitt ME110 light bomber flying over Poland, 1940. Raids by Messerschmitts, Junkers, Heinkels, and Dorniers crippled cities and destroyed factories throughout Europe.

The war was already a lost cause, however, when Wernher von Braun (*right*) developed the V1 and V2. The V2 (*above*) was packed with high explosive, and flew faster than the speed of sound from its base in Cuxhaven. For a while in late 1944 and 1945, V2s caused havoc in Antwerp and London, and dealt a serious blow to British morale. (*Far right*) The *Graf Spee*, one of the earliest casualties of war. The battleship was scuttled by the captain in Montevideo harbour, 20 December 1939.

Few Europeans could escape the effects of the Second World War. As the tide turned against Germany, day and night bombing raids rained death in ever-increasing instalments on German towns and villages. By 1945, invading armies from east and west brought even greater destruction. (*Left*) Women and children flee through the streets of a German town during a raid, April 1945.

Despite the efforts of women war workers (*right*), German planes, tanks and ships were destroyed faster than they could be replaced. Time and supplies began to run out. (*Above*) German soldiers and civilians fling themselves to the ground as shells fall on a farmhouse nearby, 24 March 1945. The last few weeks of war presented horror on an unparalleled scale to the entire country.

The advance through northern France by French, American and British armies accelerated in the late summer of 1944. By August, German troops were having to surrender in large numbers, using any vehicle that came to hand to reach Allied lines. (*Above*) A Volkswagen flying the white flag and the Red Cross brings German prisoners-of-war to the town of Trun. (*Left*) A citizen of Toulon lashes out at a German POW as he hurries to a camp, 1945. (*Opposite*) Hans-Georg Henke, a fifteen-year-old German soldier, weeps after being captured by the US 9th Army, April 1945. No one seems to have asked if his tears were of relief, fear, shame, simple exhaustion, or all of these.

(*Left*) One of the most famous images of the Second World War. The Red Flag flies over the ruins of the Berlin Reichstag, 30 April 1945. The photographer was Yevgeny Khaldei. (*Top*) The border between the Russian and American sectors of Berlin, 1 May 1949 – the day the Berlin blockade came to an end. (*Above*) A workman paints the borderline between the British and Russian zones, Potsdamer Strasse, August 1948. Disputes had arisen as to who had authority to deal with black marketeers.

By 1945 the people of Germany had suffered twelve years of Nazi rule and almost six years of war. The victors – and many Germans – believed it was time for 're-education'. (*Above, left*) Citizens of Ludwigslust see the horrors of the Wobbelin concentration camp, 7 May 1945. (*Below, left*) Some of the principal defendants at the Nuremberg War Trials, 1946. (*Opposite, above*) 'All Nazi books must be returned at once', says the note on the school blackboard of the 1st Berlin Volksschule. (*Opposite, below left*) East Berliners visit the American sector to buy Western newspapers, September 1948. (*Opposite, below right*) Josef Wagner of Bavaria studies at a POW class in England, re-learning German history, April 1946.

Berliners living in temporary Nissen huts (*above*) tend their vegetable garden, 2 September 1946. Almost every available plot of land was cultivated in the months immediately following the Second World War. Food was in short supply and there were problems bringing produce from country to the city. (*Left*) Children enjoy their dinner at a school in Dusseldorf, 1946. For many it was their only meal of the day. (*Opposite*) One of a collection of photographs taken by Fred Ramage in Berlin immediately after the war. Families plant seed potatoes in their allotments in the Tiergarten, 29 May 1946. In the background is the burnt-out shell of the Reichstag.

Destruction…furniture is removed from bombed houses in Rostock (*above, left*), 2 March 1944. Ruins…a refreshment stall does brisk business in the rubble-strewn streets of Brunswick (*below, left*). Salvage…old bricks are fed into a cleaning machine (*below, right*) before being wheeled in a trolley back to a building site. Rebuilding…seventy-six-year-old Gustav Piltz and his seventy-two-year-old wife Alma Piltz (*opposite*) help to rebuild Dresden, 1946.

(*Left*) Families in Magdeburg queue for water from a pump in the early days of Allied occupation, 1945. (*Below*) Men and children wade through the River Elbe to reach the outfall from pumps operated by dredgers. They are scavenging for lumps of coal and coke which have fallen from barges in the Hamburg Docks.

Survival was a desperate struggle. The essentials of life were scarce and access to adequate food, water and fuel was often a matter of individual cunning and persistence. Anything else was a luxury, to be bartered for coffee, sugar or cheese. (*Right*) Citizens of Hanover loot a warehouse, after the town had been captured by the US 9th Army, 19 April 1945.

As the war neared its end and for months afterwards, millions of Germans were on the move – marching to battle, fleeing from the invaders, struggling to find their way back home; looking for work, loved ones, a better life. All travelled hopefully, but relatively few had a happy homecoming. (*Opposite, above left*) Citizens of Aachen leave their streets of destruction to seek shelter behind the Allied lines, October 1944. (*Opposite, below left*) A family in Mönchengladbach use a handcart in their search for shelter, 6 March 1945. (*Opposite, below right*) Refugees crowd one of the few trains running in the last weeks of the war, while others (*above*) use centuries-old means of transport to escape the approaching invaders.

(*Left*) Soviet troops gather round an impromptu market stall near the Reichstag, Berlin, 1945. The salesman was probably a black marketeer, but could be an innocent citizen, selling his last few possessions for his family's survival. (*Below*) Allied troops swarm round what is almost certainly a black market 'pitch' near the Reichstag, August 1945. The photographer was Fred Ramage.

A special edition of *Die Neue Zeitung* (*right*) announces the issue of a new *Deutsche Mark* in the British, American and French sectors of Berlin, 24 June 1948. Shops selling essential goods were ordered to stay open. The few existing luxury stores and clubs were allowed to close. (*Below*) Vegetables are piled high in Hamburg market, 23 June 1948. Although supplies were more plentiful, prices were still high.

Although much was done within a staggeringly short time to rebuild homes and restore essential services, in some cases it was years before major reconstruction works could be contemplated. Germany had suffered as no other country had ever suffered in war. (*Opposite*) A workman repairs one of the seventy huge steel nets that had been fastened over the damaged Mohne Dam after an Allied air raid during the war, 25 September 1948. Poised high above the waters of the lake, the work was extremely dangerous and required immense strength and courage. (*Above*) Floating cranes lift girders into place during the rebuilding of a bridge, 21 September 1950.

After the Russians closed the road and rail connections between Berlin and West Germany in 1948, the city was supplied by what became known as the 'Berlin Airlift'. (*Opposite*) Children watch the arrival of a US cargo plane, 24 June 1948. (*Above*) An RAF Dakota is loaded with goods for Berlin, 24 November 1948. (*Right*) Young Berliners wait at Tempelhof Airport for 'manna from heaven'.

Slowly, painfully, but oh so sweetly, the good things in life began to return. Clubs and restaurants, theatres and cinemas reopened. It was possible to buy a drink, dine out, meet a friend for an evening in town. The old Weimar days of mad excess and wild debauchery would never come back – nor, hopefully, the days of Nazi control and oppression. But, somehow, even the glimpses of clean cutlery and a dinner jacket were reassuring.

(*Opposite, above*) A mixed crowd of locals and occupiers gathers at the Jemina night-club on Nuremburger Strasse, Berlin, July 1945. (*Opposite, below*) An afternoon when the ban on 'fraternisation' had been lifted – British troops and American GIs take their local partners for a 'getting-to-know-you' dance at an open-air café in Berlin, 18 July 1945. (*Above*) Berliners cluster round the window of a restaurant to examine the menu, and to wonder at the prices. As in every country in every war throughout history, there were some who were able to stage a personal financial recovery far more quickly than most of their fellow citizens.

In 1947 a group of writers met to discuss the future of German literature. Their aim was to rid books of pompous and affected language, to create a literature of everyday speech, that revealed rather than disguised the truth. (*Opposite*) Martin Walser, author and member of *Gruppe 47*. (*Above, left to right*) Heinrich Böll, author of *Das Brot der Frühen Jahre* (*The Bread of Our Early Years*), and winner of the 1972 Nobel Prize for Literature; Ilse Alchinger and Günther Eich, also founder members of the group.

19

BEFORE THE WALL
1950–1961

(*Right*) Delegates sign the Treaty of Rome, 25 March 1957. The founder members of the European Economic Community were West Germany, France, Italy, Luxemburg, Belgium and the Netherlands. The goal was to create a 'common market' for all goods and services, but especially coal and steel. From the outset, the greatest difficulties were in establishing a common agricultural policy acceptable to all. The hidden agenda for France and West Germany was to unite European powers in a way that would prevent a repeat of the wars and horrors of the past.

With the defeat of the Third Reich, a new cast took centre-stage in West German politics. (*Opposite, above*) Theodor Heuss, founder member of the Free Democrat Party, President from 1949 to 1959. (*Opposite, below left*) Konrad Adenauer, Chancellor from 1949, with André François-Poncet, French High Commissioner in Germany, 12 April 1951. (*Opposite, below right*) Dr Kurt Schumacher, leader of the Social Democrat Party (SPD). (*Right*) The former palace of the Archbishop Electors of Cologne, then the centre of government in the new West German capital of Bonn. (*Below, left*) Canvassing for votes in the first election for ten years, 1949. (*Below, right*) Election posters for Willy Brandt and the SPD in 1961 are unhappily placed next to a road sign indicating a 'blind alley'.

(*Above*) A line of posters decorate an East Berlin street – (from left to right) Nikita Khrushchev, Soviet premier, honoured with two pictures; Walter Ulbricht, leader of the East German Communist Party and deputy premier of the GDR; Wilhelm Pieck, President of the GDR from 1949; and Otto Grotewohl, Vice-President. (*Opposite, above*) Walter Ulbricht greets Nikita Khrushchev at Schönefeld Airport, 19 May 1960. (*Opposite, below*) Walter Pieck (left) and Otto Grotewohl admire the May Day parade in the Lustgarten, 1946.

The economic recovery of West Germany left the rest of Europe breathless with envy. (*Far left*) A 220,000 volt high-tension cable in Württemberg. (*Left*) The Huckingen steel works in the Ruhr valley, August 1949. (*Below, left*) High-rise flats in the Hansa district of West Berlin, c. 1960. (*Below, right*) German Vice-Chancellor Dr Bluegher and Ludwig Erhard, Minister for Economics, at a reception in the German Embassy, London, 13 May 1953.

(*Right and below*) The Volkswagen production lines, c. 1960. By the mid-1950s there were over a million Beetles on the roads of more than a hundred countries. The factory at Wolfsburg employed 28,000 people and turned out 1,230 cars a day. The basic working week was 42.5 hours, and the workers were paid 2.53DM per hour. They also had three weeks' paid holiday each year.

The division of Germany into two separate states was not the most astute political move in the 20th century. Families and communities were divided. The West German shop window of capitalism turned Reds green with envy in East Germany. (*Above, left*) Soviet tanks disperse thousands of workers who supported the strike at the Stalinallee construction site in East Berlin, 18 June 1953. More than four hundred people were killed in the conflict. (*Below, left*) Columbus House in the Potsdamer Platz burns the following day.

(*Right*) Demonstrators at the Brandenburg Gate early in the riots of June 1953, and (*far right*) on the anti-government march that led to the declaration of martial law. (*Below*) After the riots of June, citizens of East Berlin continued to enter West Berlin as often as possible, to collect free food distributed by US authorities. The American motives may have been humanitarian or mischievous, but the food tasted good either way.

(*Opposite, above*) Stalin-allee, from the corner of Andreastrasse, running east through Berlin. (*Opposite, below left*) Students from the Palucca ballet school in Dresden help to bring in the harvest, 12 September 1962. (*Opposite, below right*) East Berliners stash food distributed by the US in the bottom of a baby carriage. (*Right*) East German farmers on their own land, with the former stately home of a Grosen-heim landowner in the background.

After the restrictions placed on art by the Nazi authorities, artists enjoyed a new freedom in post-war Germany. (*Above, left*) The Austrian painter Oskar Kokoschka at work in his studio, 1961. (*Below, left*) President Theodor Heuss and Professor Arnold Bode (left) in front of a Picasso canvas at the documenta Exhibition, Kassel, 16 September 1955.

The German painter and sculptor Max Ernst (*right*) at London's Tate Gallery, September 1961. Many of his earlier works were destroyed by the Nazis. (*Below, left*) George Grosz returns to Germany after twenty-five years in America, 8 June 1959. (*Below, right*) Hans Arp, one of the founders of the Dada movement, with a typical piece of organic abstract sculpture.

Nr. 325. Hermann Hesse.
Eigh. Gedicht.

FRANKFURTER
BUCHMESSE 1961
23. OKTOBER AUF DEM MESSEGELÄNDE
MIT REPRÄSENTATIVEN AUSSTELLUNGEN
AUSLÄNDISCHER VERLAGE

(*Above, left*) Hermann Hesse, the poet, novelist and essayist who was awarded the Nobel Prize for Literature in 1946. (*Above, right*) The manuscript copy of Hesse's poem *Spring*. (*Left*) The smallest book in the world is exhibited at the inaugural Frankfurt Book Fair, 17 October 1961. More than thirty countries contributed books to the Fair, which subsequently became one of the biggest in the world.

German literary giants from the post-war period: (*clockwise, from top left*) Hermann Kesten, novelist; Gottfried Benn, who regained critical acclaim with *Statische Gedichte*, a volume of poems published in 1948, and his autobiography *Doppelleben*, published in 1950; Erich Kästner, author of children's books in the 1930s, who wrote his autobiography in 1957; and Paul Celan, whose first volume of poetry, *Der Sand aus den Urnen*, was published in 1948.

The old guard of German musical talent was quickly joined by a new generation of musicians.
(*Opposite*) Wolfgang Sawallisch conducts a recording of Richard Strauss's *Capriccio*, London,
6 September 1957. The singers in the booths are (left to right) Dietrich Fischer-Dieskau, Hans Hotter,
Eberhard Wächter, Christa Ludwig and Elisabeth Schwarzkopf. The photograph is by Erich Auerbach.
(*Above, left*) The soprano Elisabeth Schwarzkopf studies a score. (*Above, right*) Paul Hindemith,
composer of *Mathis der Maler*, *Symphonic Metamorphosis of Themes by Weber* and *Die Harmonie der Welt*,
at a press conference in Munich, 7 August 1957.

The waves of American invasions washed against the shores of Europe throughout the 1950s – food, films, clothes and (most powerfully of all) music. (*Clockwise from top*) German youth – the best-fed generation of all time – at a Fifties concert; a couple dancing at the first record hop held in Germany, 26 June 1959; and teenagers scream their approval of Bill Haley and the Comets at a performance in the Berlin Sportpalast, 26 October 1958. (*Opposite*) An athletic display of jitterbugging at a youth club in Kreuzberg, 12 December 1962.

(*Opposite*) The actor and theatre director Gustav Gründgens as Mephisto in a performance of Goethe's *Faust* at the Deutsches Schauspielhaus, Hamburg, 1959. (*Above, left*) Therese Giehse and Siegfried Lowitz in a moment of terror from *The Rats* at the Münchener Kammerspiele, 1952. (*Above, right*) Stars of the new German cinema – Lili Palmer, as the cruel egotistical wife, and Curd Jürgens, as her weak musician husband, in *The Devil in Silk*, January 1956.

German cinema rapidly re-established itself with a series of popular films that tended to concentrate on the lighter side of life. (*Opposite*) The comedian Heinz Erhardt stars in *The Stolen Pair of Trousers*, 1956. (*Above*) A production still on the set of *Der Hauptmann von Köpenick*, a film version of an event that took place in the 1900s when a cobbler successfully imitated an army captain – to the delight of the Kaiser and the general public. The film was made in 1956 and starred Heinz Rühmann.

German drivers and German cars had considerable success on the Grand Prix circuits of the world in the 1950s and 1960s, but there were times when the sport itself was called into question. (*Above*) A poignant photograph of the racing ace Wolfgang von Trips at the wheel of his Ferrari on the track at Monza, 10 September 1961. The picture was taken just before the crash in which von Trips and fourteen spectators were killed.

It had taken a little while for the top German racing-car stables to produce a new generation of cars. The first time German cars competed in a Grand Prix race was on 17 July 1954, when Mercedes entered a team for the French Grand Prix at Reims. (*Above*) The old master, Alfred Neubauer, instructs a mechanic to signal to the two Mercedes taking part. Neubauer returned to the track after an absence of fifteen years.

New prosperity opened up new horizons for millions of German workers and their families in the 1950s. The automobile society had the means to get out and about for their holidays. (*Opposite*) Camping in Melbeck, near Lüneburg, 30 April 1961. The Camping Club of Germany organised a mass outing for over a thousand people. (*Above, left*) New mobility brought with it new traffic queues – drivers wait patiently by their cars to pass the checkpoint on the way from West Berlin to the Federal Republic, 12 July 1958. (*Above, right*) Another way, another obstacle. Young hikers wait for a ferry to cross the Rhine to the castle of Pfalz Grafenstein, near Kaub, 12 August 1960.

A machine for every purpose... (*Left*) A woman gazes, perhaps in wonder and appreciation, at an automatic vending machine, 1955. (*Opposite, clockwise from top left*) A passenger at Tempelhof Airport braves the coffee dispensed by the 'robot' in a departure lounge; a Telefunken TV set designed by Hans Gugelot and Helmut Mueller, 30 April 1958; the Messerschmitt 'bubble car' on a London street, 1955; and a carbonic acid atomiser for spraying the teeth clean, 1957.

FEINKOST

(*Above, left*) Sixteen-year-old-student designer Karl Lagerfeld from Hamburg with the coat he designed in 1954. The design won him first prize in an international fashion competition and was later taken up by Pierre Balmain. (*Above, right*) A Fifties full skirt aids 'lift-off' to clear a Munich puddle, 22 April 1960. (*Opposite, clockwise from top left*) Not the best fashion accessory on a hot day, No. 1 – a dachshund; not the best fashion accessory for a hot day, No. 2 – woollen wigs; three smart actresses at a Berlin café, 21 April 1958; and what the well-dressed Munich secretary was wearing, 27 October 1960.

20
RESTLESS ADVANCE
1961–1968

It began in August 1961, when East German border guards placed rolls of barbed wire along the line separating East and West Berlin. Within a fortnight a wall of concrete blocks, shoulder high, had been erected. There was to be no more slipping from one ideology to another – at least, not as far as communism was concerned. Russian and American tanks faced each other where the Wall was incomplete. Guards on both sides were heavily armed. It was a breathless moment for the whole world. (*Left*) Sightseers arrive by bus for a glimpse of East Berlin, 19 February 1964.

Introduction

On 15 August 1961, a nineteen-year-old East German border guard named Conrad Schumann leapt over the barbed wire that separated East and West Berlin. During the next few weeks he discovered a city, and a country, in the throes of change. From the moment that the GDR had erected the wall in 1961 the United States had hurried to the aid of West Germany. They were given a mixed reception. Politicians of the Centre and Right were glad to have allies by their side in the increasingly frigid stand-off against Communism. Students and left-wing intellectuals, however, were strongly critical of US interference. More welcome was the Franco-German Treaty of 1963.

Adenauer – now labelled 'der Alte' – resigned two years later, in 1963. His place was taken by Ludwig Erhard, who hoped to establish better relations between East and West and advocated 'capitalism with a heart'. To which end, Erhard's Foreign Minister, Gerhard Schroeder, approved trade treaties with Poland, Hungary, Bulgaria and Romania. The rise and rise of German industry continued, with production in the West almost doubling in value in the 1960s, and the 'super-workers' of the GDR claiming to have achieved much the same result. Erhard also proposed that *Länder* (except the GDR) should renounce the use of force and strictly limit the numbers of nuclear weapons.

But protest was as angry in West Germany in the 1960s as it was in France, Britain and the United States. In 1962 the *Der Spiegel* affair rocked Adenauer's government. The magazine published an article pointing out a number of deficiencies in West Germany's defences. Franz Josef Strauss, the Minister of Defence, accused the magazine of betraying State secrets. There were arrests. The magazine's offices were raided. Later, Franz Josef Strauss admitted he had 'acted somewhat outside the law' in demanding the arrests.

To a generation born just before and during the war this smacked of State bullying, recreating the nightmare of the Nazi years. It was all very well President Kennedy proudly proclaiming 'Ich bin ein Berliner'. Was the same true of his successor, Lyndon Johnson? And, if so, what was 'ein Berliner' doing involving American troops in the Vietnam War? Within a couple of years sit-ins, teach-ins, strikes and even riots became unofficial components of university and college curricula. 'Beautiful people' formed communes in the West. Hard-working people formed collectives in the East. Rudi Dutschke fanned the fires of protest. Water cannon quenched the flames. The 'Extra-Parliamentary Opposition' (APO) was born.

Meanwhile, on the other side of the Wall, Chancellor Walter Ulbricht was determined that 'while everything should look democratic, we must be in control'.

The first to cross the embryonic Wall was a nineteen-year-old East German soldier, who leapt over the wire on 12 August 1961 (*above, left*). Peter Leibing's camera recorded the moment. As tension eased and the Wall became a familiar object, Berliners learnt to live with the monstrosity in the heart of their city. (*Below, left*) Families and friends wave to one another over the Wall.

Though without the blessings of Coca-Cola, the East German authorities had plenty of barbed wire with which to 'protect' the Russian sector (*above*), 20 August 1961. (*Right*) On Bornauer Strasse, a West Berlin daughter waves to her mother who lives in East Berlin. (*Far right*) Unplagued by through traffic, a family settles down to enjoy a spring picnic beside the Berlin Wall, 27 May 1964.

For many years Berlin remained the focal point of the Cold War, the likely flashpoint for conflict between East and West. As such, the city attracted many politicians and world leaders. (*Above*) West German President Heinrich Lübke greets Charles de Gaulle, President of France, in Bonn at the beginning of a six-day visit, 4 September 1962. (*Right*) President John F. Kennedy of the United States with Willy Brandt (centre), Mayor of West Berlin, and Chancellor Konrad Adenauer, 26 June 1963. Kennedy stayed just over seven hours in the city, announcing 'Ich bin ein Berliner'.

Thousands of young Germans gathered to protest at Soviet treatment of Czechoslovakia during the Prague Spring of 1968. (*Above, left*) Red flags are burnt in West Berlin, 21 August 1968. (*Below, left*) Crowds outside the Soviet Embassy in Bonn two nights later. (*Above, right*) The student leader, Rudi Dutschke, delivers a fiery message to a meeting in Frankfurt, 5 February 1968.

(*Above*) Students gather at Munich University to demand the resignation of the German Minister of Defence, Franz Josef Strauss, 12 November 1962. The demand arose out of the *Der Spiegel* affair. After the magazine published an article pointing out deficiencies in West Germany's defence system, its offices were raided and its staff arrested. It was subsequently shown that Strauss had lied to the Bundestag, but he refused to resign, though parliamentary custom demanded that he should. The government coalition collapsed, and no place was found for Strauss in the replacement government.

Although there were frequent 'incidents' on the border between East and West Germany, most Germans took the division in their stride. (*Above, left*) An unconcerned sunbather on Priwaller Strand near Travemünde, 25 August 1966, and (*above, right*) a family picnicking on the same beach earlier that year. (*Left*) A farm cart brings in the harvest under West German police protection, 20 August 1953.

(*Above*) Guests at the Hohegeiss in the Harz Mountains enjoy fresh air and a view across the Iron Curtain, 19 May 1961. (*Right*) Inhabitants of Niedergandern, West Germany, serenade their friends in the nearby village of Kirchgandern, East Germany, 6 November 1961. Wire and guards keep the two communities apart.

Fire and water have brought tragedy to the citizens of Hamburg in two terrifying disasters in the 20th century. On 28 July 1943 it became the first German city to suffer a firestorm. Incendiary and high explosive bombs dropped by allied planes caused a 20-square-kilometre conflagration in the centre of the city, which in turn created hurricane-strength winds that uprooted trees and sucked people into the inferno. It is estimated that some 45,000 people died that night.

Nineteen years later water brought havoc to the city. Hurricane-force winds whipped the sea over the coastal defences (*opposite*), and the River Elbe burst its banks. Three hundred and fifteen people were drowned – two hundred of them in the Wilhelmsburg district alone – on the night of 16 February 1962. (*Above*) Rescuers use small boats to bring stranded residents to safety.

(*Opposite, above left*) One of the new wave of German conductors – Erich Auerbach's study of Rudolf Kempe, 14 June 1961. (*Opposite, above right*) Herbert von Karajan, new master of the Berlin Philharmonic Orchestra. (*Opposite, below*) The piano virtuoso Wilhelm Kempff – another photograph by Erich Auerbach. (*Above, right*) Dietrich Fischer-Dieskau as Falstaff, and (*below, right*) performing in Benjamin Britten's *War Requiem* in Coventry Cathedral, 1962. (*Below, left*) Karl Böhm, conductor of the Vienna Philharmonic Orchestra.

(*Opposite, above left*) Customers are taken in hand at a Munich bar in the Sixties. (*Opposite, above right*)
The actress Hildegard Knef in the role of Trilby O'Ferrall for the Renown Pictures production of
Svengali, 1954. (*Opposite, below*) The top model they called 'The Animal' – Veruschka (real name Vera,
Gräfin von Lehndorff) – poses for the world's cameras at Sydney Airport in the 1960s. (*Above, left*)
Another airport, another star – the German actress Senta Berger at Rome's Fiumicino Airport, 23 July
1965. (*Above, right*) Elke Sommer photographed by Erich Auerbach on 12 January 1963.

(*Opposite*) East Berlin guards supervise the rebuilding of part of the Berlin Wall after an explosion removed two metres of the concrete monstrosity near the corner of Bernauer Strasse and Schwadter Strasse, 26 May 1962. The Wall hindered, but could not prevent, escapes. (*Right*) A former East Berliner arrives by rope in West Berlin. Though a relatively simple method of escape, it was highly dangerous. The guards had orders to shoot any would-be escapees.

21
LEVELLING OFF
1968–1975

It had been the Final the whole world wanted to see – the dedicated West Germans against Holland, the team committed to the new concept of 'Total Football'. In the end, West Germany won by two goals to one, although Holland had started with the fastest goal in any World Cup Final, and without Germany touching the ball. Then Breitner converted a penalty, and Gerd Müller scored the winning goal. (*Left*) West Germany's captain Franz Beckenbauer and coach Helmut Schön in celebratory mood after the final whistle at the Olympic Stadium in Munich, 7 July 1974.

Introduction

In the eyes of the rest of the world, the two Germanys had developed in increasingly divergent directions since the end of the Second World War. In the East, the satellite status forced on the GDR by the Soviet Union had resulted in full employment, low rents and security of tenure at the cost of propping up outdated methods of production and subsidising industries that filled the skies and streams of Eastern Europe with toxic pollution.

In the West, the Federal Republic had become the economic envy of the whole of Europe. Wages were high, production was at record levels. The citizens of West Germany owned fine flats and houses, drove fine cars, travelled freely throughout the world, and enjoyed one of the highest standards of living. To most West Germans there had been no accompanying drawbacks, but in the late 1960s and early 1970s there emerged pockets of rampant discontent. Left-wing students saw the

Federal Republic as little more than a satellite of the United States, a militarised buffer zone created and held to halt the spread of Communism. Some carried their discontent to violent levels; many more took their feelings on to the streets, their anger reaching its peak following the shooting of a student during a demonstration in West Berlin in 1968. A militant few – notably the Baader–Meinhof gang – embarked on a programme of extreme direct action.

But a calmer atmosphere was created by two events. Leaders of the USA and the USSR sought to ease the tension between East and West (including that between East and West Germany), and Willy Brandt formed a coalition government of members of the SPD and the FDP. To a degree, Brandt's *Ostpolitik* followed the American line. It was greeted coldly by the East German government until Moscow replaced Walter Ulbricht with Erich Honecker as party leader. In

May 1973, Brandt and Honecker ratified a formal treaty between the two Germanys, the first in which both recognised the other's existence.

There were still those who were prepared to try any means of escape to the West from the East – a group of fifty-seven crossed from East to West Berlin by tunnel in 1964, and one couple made the journey by balloon in the early 1970s – but the gap between the two countries was steadily narrowing.

In sport both countries continued to excel. Between them they won ten gold medals at the Mexico Olympics in 1968, and twenty-eight gold medals at the Munich Olympics in 1972. Only the superpowers could do better. Borussia Dortmund won the European Cup Winners' Cup in 1966, Bayern Munich won the same cup the following year and the European Cup in 1974 and 1975. The crowning football glory was the West German victory in the World Cup Final in 1974.

(*Opposite*) Karl Herbert Frahm (better known as 'Willy Brandt') (right) pursues his *Ostpolitik* in the Soviet Union, 17 September 1971. With him, in rare jovial mood, is Leonid Brezhnev. (*Below, right*) Chancellor Willy Brandt and East German Prime Minister Willi Stoph meet across the table, 19 March 1970. They queue to get in... (*above, left*) West Germans wait patiently in their cars to visit East Berlin, 25 December 1971...and they queue to get out... (*above, right*) Refugees from East Germany crowd into a reception centre in West Berlin. By the 1970s the flow of refugees was over 1,000 per day.

(*Opposite, clockwise from top left*) President Gustav Heinemann of West Germany with Queen Juliana, during a state visit to the Netherlands, 25 November 1969; Chancellor Helmut Schmidt, 1974; Ralf Dahrendorf, Director of the London School of Economics, 3 October 1974; and Annemarie Renger of the SPD. (*Above, right*) (from left to right) Harold Wilson, Prime Minister of Britain, with President Gerald Ford of the USA, President Valéry Giscard D'Estaing of France and Chancellor Helmut Schmidt of West Germany, 2 August 1975. (*Below, right*) Walter Scheel, former President of the Federal Republic, on holiday with his children in the late 1970s.

The Red Army Faction was a terrorist group founded by Andreas Baader (*far left*) and Ulrike Meinhof (*left*) in the early 1970s. Their aim was to expose by violent means what they saw as the lurking fascism of the consumer society. It didn't work. Public opinion was strongly against them and their methods, and they drew support from just a few disillusioned members of the middle class – among them (*below*) Irene Goergens (left), Ingrid Schubert and their lawyer, Horst Mahler.

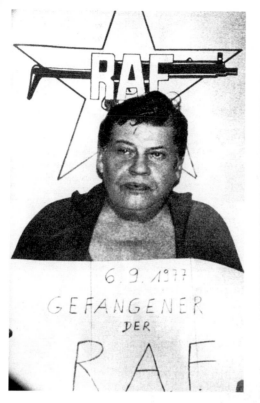

One of the Red Army Faction's kidnap victims, Hans-Martin Schleyer (*above, left*) was President of the Federal Association of German Industry. The photograph was released on 6 September 1977 to prove that he was still alive. (*Above, right*) One of the Black September guerrillas who broke into the Munich Olympic village in September 1972 and took nine Israeli athletes hostage. All the hostages and all but three of the gang were killed in a shoot-out at Munich Airport.

The writing was on the wall for the traditional industries of Germany. In the East, old methods of production were maintained – with all the accompanying pollution. In the West, changes had to be made. (*Opposite, above*) German and visiting workers at a Daimler-Benz car plant, 1972. (*Opposite, below*) A lignite strip mine near Cologne, c. 1972. (*Above, left*) Dirty chimneys – the new enemy. Factories belch pollution into the skies above the Ruhr valley in the early 1970s. (*Above, right*) Clean funnels – an old friend: painters at work on the funnel of a ship docked in Hamburg, 22 November 1969.

(*Clockwise from top left*) Hanna Schygulla; Romy Schneider as Leni in the Orson Welles version of Kafka's *The Trial*; Klaus Kinski in the spaghetti Western *Three Against the Devil*, 1972; and Hardy Krüger as *Potato Fritz*, 1976.

(*Above, right*) The producer–director Rainer Werner Fassbinder with the actress Rosel Zech watching rushes of *Die Sehnsucht der Veronika Voss*, 1981. (*Below, right*) The French director Louis Malle (left) with the German director Volker Schlöndorff discuss their joint production, *Lacombe Lucien*, 8 March 1974.

The path blazed by Schönberg, Webern and Berg led eventually to Karlheinz Stockhausen (*above*) and Hans Werner Henze (*opposite*). Both had their critics and detractors, both had their champions and their admirers. It was not always easy to know where electrophonic music was going (or where it had been). Stockhausen, it was said, 'often engages in formidably technical discussions of the scientific basis of his art, in terms not always understood by trained physicists'. Henze's music is more accessible, and his operas attract large audiences.

Post-war ballet has established one of its most secure footholds in Germany, and foremost among its ballet companies is the Stuttgart Ballet, presided over by John Cranko in the 1960s. (*Right*) Donald MacLeary (left), Marcia Haydee and Anthony Dowell perform *Song of the Earth*, to music by Gustav Mahler. Marcia Haydee took over from Cranko as ballet director, and was also prima ballerina.

(*Above*) The equestrian champion Alwin Schockemöhle and his mount Donald Rex clear one of the jumps at the men's European showjumping championship, Hickstead, England, 17 July 1969. (*Opposite, above*) A day at the races...the field of horses rounds a bend on the Iffezheim course near Baden-Baden. (*Opposite, below*) Traditional horsemanship...a four-horse carriage competes at an equestrian meeting at Aachen, 1972.

Greater prosperity meant more opportunities to enjoy life for the average German in the 1970s. (*Above, left*) Holidaymakers on the beach at Sylt, 1978. (*Below, left*) Sailing on the River Alster on the outskirts of Hamburg. (*Below, right*) A young reveller enjoys the carnival, 1972. (*Opposite, above*) Adults test their courage and their stomachs on the chair-o-planes at a Munich amusement park, 1980. (*Opposite, below*) Senior citizens on an excursion through Goslar, 1972. Both photographs on this page are by Ernst Haas.

22
THE WALL COMES DOWN 1975–1989

The Berlin Wall became the most hated border in the world. Over the twenty-eight years of its existence at least eighty people were killed trying to cross it, but hundreds succeeding in outwitting or outrunning the authorities guarding it. There were escapes by submarine, hot air balloon, tunnels, gliders, and even in the stomach of a pantomime cow. Eventually, the stupidity and the inhumanity of maintaining such an obstacle to free movement within a single city gave way to public protest, and the Wall came down. (*Left*) A month after the first breach of the Wall, 100,000 demonstrators gather on the Wall and the Brandenburg Gate, New Year's Eve, 1989.

Introduction

In 1982 Helmut Kohl, newly appointed Chancellor of West Germany, remarked: 'The German nation is divided. The German nation remains and will continue to exist. We all know that the end to this division can only be conceived in terms of historical epochs.' It was an oft-repeated premise in the history of Germany, but what neither Kohl, nor his East German counterpart Erich Honecker, nor indeed the vast majority of Germans knew was how close their country was to a new epoch.

The signs were there. An acceleration of the arms race and a new generation of weapons of mass destruction had made it imperative that East and West Germany come to some peaceful accord. For the first time there was official opposition to the presence of NATO in the Federal Republic. Like his predecessor Willy Brandt, Kohl was forced to pay heed to the 'issue' politicians of the day, for there were twenty-eight Green Party members of the Federal Parliament in 1983.

Across the border, the East German economy

was crippled by the ever-increasing expense of its welfare state. In 1971 the annual government subsidy for food, industrial production and wages had been 8,500 million marks. By 1988 it had soared to 50,000 million marks. During the same period, the price of imported raw materials had risen by 300 per cent, while the value of exported goods had risen by only 130 per cent.

Many of the best and worst events of history are the result of panic. In 1983 Franz Josef Strauss, a bitter opponent of socialism, helped negotiate a 2,000 million DM loan from the Federal Republic to the GDR. Slowly, the ideological gap between East and West began to narrow, as Honecker embarked on a series of policies that owed more to Western consumerism than to Marxist-Leninism. Cars and television sets rolled off production lines, and for a year or so freedom of expression raised its dangerous head. The enforced exile of the East German singer Wolf Biermann signalled the end of this period, and provoked a storm of protest. In Leipzig over 120,000 people demonstrated against the Communist regime.

It was a taste of what was to come, and a flavour of what was already happening in neighbouring countries. Solidarity had broken the hard-line government in Poland. Hungary's barbed-wire border with Austria was dismantled in May 1989. Six months later, the Czechoslovakian Communist Party lost its forty-one-year-old monopoly on power. The same month a million East Berliners demonstrated for free elections, freedom of expression, and freedom to travel beyond their socialist boundaries.

And then, the unthinkable happened. Crowds gathered on either side of the Berlin Wall. Whatever the reasons had been for erecting it (to protect, to shelter, to imprison, to assert), the people of Berlin, on both sides, had decided it was time for the Wall to come down...

New age politicians: (*Opposite, above*) Helmut Kohl, Chancellor of West Germany from 1982; (*opposite, below left*) Chancellor Helmut Schmidt (centre) arrives in England, 1981; (*opposite, below right*) Hans-Dieter Genscher, German Minister for Foreign Affairs at a convention in Munich, 1976. (*Right, clockwise from top left*) A traffic sign points the way to the Chancellor's Office in Bonn for Franz Josef Strauss, 1986; Richard von Weizsäcker of the CDU, 1981; Marieluise Beck-Oberdorf of the Green Party looks doubtfully at Helmut Kohl; the Green Environment Minister, Joschka Fischer, swears allegiance to the Hesse Parliament, 1985.

In the spring of 1989 Hungary opened its border with Austria. By summer one hundred and eighty GDR citizens were camping in the grounds of the West German embassy in Budapest. The movement grew. In October mass demonstrations took place in Leipzig and Dresden against the Communist regime. (*Above*) East German citizens share joy and relief at the West German embassy in Prague. (*Opposite*) Ten years earlier, Hans-Peter Strelzik, his wife Doris and their sons Frank and Andreas – with another family – escape by balloon from the GDR and land in Bavaria, 17 September 1979.

(*Opposite, above left*) With the motto 'Don't be afraid', and a slogan reading 'For a nuclear-weapon-free Europe', 130,000 anti-nuclear protesters parade in Hamburg. (*Opposite, above right*) Anti-nuclear waste demonstrators at a borehole in Gorleben, West Germany. (*Opposite, below*) Police face a section of the Gorleben crowd, 4 June 1980. (*Above right*) One of 1,500 demonstrators at the site of a proposed nuclear power plant at Brokdorf, 16 November 1976. (*Right, below*) Four months later the protest at Brokdorf had grown. Six thousand police were ordered into the area.

Germany was one European country to suffer enormously from the effects of acid rain in the 1980s and 1990s. (*Opposite*) A helicopter sprays chalk on a forest near Oldenburg, 6 October 1998. The chalk neutralises the acid and repairs some of the worst damage. (*Above*) A scientist at the GFS Research Centre for Health and the Environment in Munich analyses the effects of pollution on young pine trees. Research and measures against pollution are slow and expensive. Pollution is rapid and cheap.

Some of the stars of the German music scene in the 1980s. (*Opposite, above left*) The young violinist Anne-Sophie Mutter. (*Opposite, above right*) Kurt Masur conducting at the Old Opera House in Frankfurt, 23 April 1990. Masur was a forthright supporter of the movement to reunite Germany. (*Opposite, below*) The Hungarian soprano Eva Marton (left) as Elektra and Brigitte Fassbaender as Klytamnestra in Richard Strauss's *Elektra* at the Salzburg Festival, 9 August 1989. (*Above, left*) The German painter and sculptor Joseph Beuys, November 1985. Beuys was a founder of the Green Party in Germany. (*Above, right*) Horst Janssen, painter and graphic designer, 1987.

(*Above, left*) A group of East German performers use their music to point out the shortcomings of the political regime in the GDR. (From left) Wolf Biermann, Eva-Maria Hagen and her daughter Nina Hagen, and Ralf Hirsch. Hirsch had just been released from prison. (*Below, left*) Marius Müller-Westernhagen, rock singer with such hits as *Johnny Walker* and *Freiheit*, and star of the films *Der Schneemann* and *Theo gegen den Rest der Welt*. (*Opposite*) The singer and teenage sensation Nena, during a concert in the Offenbach Town Hall, 2 April 1984.

German cinema lost one of its greatest directors with the death of Rainer Werner Fassbinder in 1982. He had just finished two films – *Lili Marleen* and *Lola* – and was planning a series of films based on German history as seen through the eyes of women. But there was much rising talent. (*Above*) Nastassja Kinski, in the title role of Roman Polanski's 1989 production, *Tess*, based on *Tess of the D'Urbevilles* by Thomas Hardy.

(*Above*) Gudrun Landgrebe (left) and Mathieu Carriere in *Die flambierte Frau*, directed by Robert van Ackeren in 1983. The two stars played the parts of call-girl and call-boy in a film that explored some of the moral enigmas of a sexually promiscuous age.

German sports stars continued to reach the top in the last decades of the 20th century. One of the finest golfers, able to take on the best in the world, was Bernhard Langer – here competing in the British Open golf championship at Sandwich in Kent, England, 21 July 1981.

(*Above, left*) Boris Becker was a product of the German tennis league system. In 1984 he hit the headlines as the seventeen-year-old runner-up in the US Open. A year later he became the youngest player ever to win the men's singles championship at the All England Club, Wimbledon. (*Above, right*) Anything Becker could do, Steffi Graf could do better. With a staggering technique and an amazing speed on court, Graf won the grand slam of women's tournaments in 1988 – the US, Australian, French and Wimbledon competitions – and all at the age of nineteen.

(*Left*) Andreas Brehme of West Germany leaps past a Mexican defender during the World Cup quarter-final in Monterey, Mexico, 21 June 1986. West Germany won 4-1 on penalties, went on to beat France in the semi-final, but lost to Argentina in the Final.

(*Right*) World Cup semi-final 1982. The French forward Jean Tigana stretches to tackle Paul Breitner in Seville. West Germany won on penalties. (*Below, left*) Karl-Heinz Rummenigge blasts a shot at the Albanian goal. (*Below, right*) Lothar Matthäus in action during West Germany's victory over Mexico in the 1986 World Cup.

Rosi Mittermaier (*above*) competes in the Winter Olympics at Innsbruck, February 1976. She came within a hundredth of a second of winning all three women's alpine events, a breathtaking achievement. (*Opposite, below left*) Katarina Witt in action during the women's figure skating competition at the 1988 Winter Olympics in Calgary, Canada.

(*Above left*) Hans-Joachim Stuck, the German racing driver, in contemplative mood before a practice circuit at Brands Hatch, England, 16 July 1976. (*Above, right*) Ulrike Meyfarth on her way to winning the gold medal for the women's high jump at the 1984 Olympics in Los Angeles. (*Below, right*) Jürgen Hingsen during a round of the men's decathlon at the Los Angeles Olympics. He won the silver medal.

The Association for the Promotion of Munich Beer Gardens keeps up the good work in the late 20th century. (*Above*) Some of the 100,000 visitors to the *Oktoberfest* enjoy Munich's beer. (*Left*) The perfect accompaniment to Bavarian beer – a Bavarian band. Despite aggressive sales campaigns by sellers of other alcoholic drinks, beer reigns supreme in southern Germany.

(*Above*) A parade of clowns display mixed emotions at a carnival in the Rhineland. In some, the spirit of Pagliacci appears nearer tears than laughter. (*Right*) Old masks on parade in the *Rottweiler Narrensprung* on the 'Dirty Thursday' preceding *Fasching* weekend. The poles have a dual use – as bars over which to jump, and as rods for fighting.

(*Above, left*) East Germans celebrate the end of an era on top of the Berlin Wall, New Year's Eve 1989. (*Below, left*) West Berliners and hundreds of visitors gaze down into East Berlin. (*Opposite, clockwise from top left*) Hammering home the message – a young East German widens the crack in the Wall...until it is wide enough to peer through; the remains of the wall are decorated with a picture of Leonid Brezhnev embracing Erich Honecker, 1993; and a wrecked Trabant in East Berlin. The East German regime had ground to a halt.

23
GERMANY UNITED
1989–2000

The Soviet Union's military presence in Germany came to an end and the last Russian troops prepared to leave Berlin, 31 August 1994. Boris Yeltsin and Helmut Kohl, together with Russian and German soldiers, met to commemorate the millions of their countrymen and women who died in the Second World War. It was a time for sober reflection and optimistic determination. (*Right*) A Berlin woman gives a Russian officer a farewell kiss.

Introduction

When the two Germanys were reunited in 1989, it was not a marriage of equal partners. On one side of the Wall there was BMWs, material plenty and a well-ordered and well-maintained environment. On the other side there were Trabants, shortages, and a chokingly polluted environment.

What was to become of such a union? There were some who disapproved of the whole idea (among them the novelist Günther Grass). Some West Germans feared the assimilation of East Germany could only be achieved at the expense of their own jobs, houses and standard of living. Some East Germans opposed the idea of abandoning socialism – though their voices were raised in somewhat muted protest for the time being. Others anticipated the creation of a 'Two Nation' state, fundamentally a land of the 'haves' and 'have-nots'. Critics and cynics pointed out that such a dichotomy had always been true of the GDR – a land where party officials could jump any queue, buy Western cars and shop at the Exquisit and Delikat stores for luxuries that were denied the masses.

In August 1989, before the formal dismantling of the Wall, East German refugees pouring over the Hungarian frontier into Austria and on into West Germany had been greeted ecstatically. But the movement outgrew the available hospitality, just at the moment in East Germany when people were demanding that the government examine why so many of its citizens wished to leave – rather than spend valuable energy and resources trying to prevent the leaving.

Once the Wall was down, and the rest of the border had been opened, the stream of refugees flowed from east to west at the rate of between 1,000 and 2,000 each day – a third of a million in a year. The pace of change quickened. Egon Krenz, who had replaced Erich Honecker, was in turn replaced by Gregor Gysi as leader of the SED, which now called itself the 'Party of Democratic Socialism'. It made little difference. Far more important was the currency union of East and West Germany on 1 July 1990. By 3 October the GDR had ceased to exist, and Germany had been reunited.

If a symbol was needed to mark the historical importance of this event, it came with the completion of British architect Norman Foster's new Reichstag building. The national pain and anguish of partition was over. In the one hundred and thirty years since the modern German nation had been proclaimed in the Palace of Versailles, its people had endured two prolonged, bitter and horribly destructive wars, subjugation to a brutal and internationally vilified dictatorship, and enforced separation.

While all this was going on, Germans continued to enrich their own lives – and those of the rest of the world – scientifically, commercially, artistically and in sport. In that may lie some measure of the greatness of the German people.

(*Left*) Chancellor Gerhard Schröder of the Social Democrat Party and his Foreign Minister Joschka Fischer of the Greens, new leaders of the newly reunited Germany. It had taken almost half a century to bring the division of Germany to an end. The process was hastened by the collapse of the Soviet Union and the desire of many Western politicians to unite Germany, but the expressed will of the people played an enormous part in the extraordinary events from 1989 onwards. (*Above*) Rabbi Joel Berger attaches the *Mezuza* to the wall of the new office of the *Zentralrat* of Jews in Berlin. In the foreground on the left is Ignatz Bubis, head of the *Zentralrat*, and on the left Roman Herzog, President of Germany.

In a world of fast food and canned drink, many still favoured the traditional fare of Germany. (*Above*) Women free a catch of herring from the fishermen's nets in Mecklenburg-West. (*Left*) A flock of *Heidschnucken* sheep graze on the rich pastureland of Lüneburg Heath. The sheep are descended from the *mouflon* of Corsica.

(*Above*) A series of terraced vineyards in the Saale-Unstrut wine-making area of central Germany. The area produces five main varieties of grape: Müller-Thurgau, Silvaner, Morio-Muskat, Weissburgunder and Riesling.

(*Right*) A woman cuts a cabbage from a field in the Fildern – a high, fertile plain to the south of Stuttgart. White cabbage has been grown here since the 16th century, when the monks of Denkendorf began its cultivation.

(*Above*) The 'Manhattan' skyline of Frankfurt-am-Main, Hessew, commercial centre of modern Germany and home to more than four hundred banks. Its importance as a trading centre began in Roman times as a river crossing point and junction between north and south Germany. (*Left*) Dealing on the Frankfurt Stock Exchange in the 1990s.

(*Above*) A worker spray-paints a new model at the Porsche factory in Stuttgart, Baden-Württemberg, a car centre that rivals Detroit. The city has the highest general standard of prosperity in Germany. (*Right*) Installing research equipment into a dummy that will be used to test safety design and equipment at the Volkswagen plant.

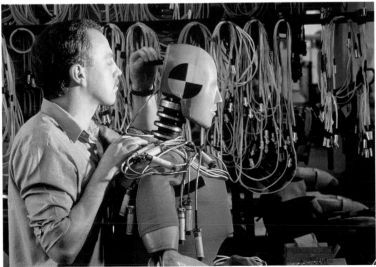

After leading the world in so many areas of design, modern Germany has developed a fashion industry to rival those of Milan, Paris or London. (*Above*) Fashion designer Jil Sander at her office desk, 1983.

One of the most famous models in the world – Claudia Schiffer poses for the news cameras at a *prêt-à-porter* fashion show of a collection by French designer Yves Saint Laurent, 17 March 1996.

(*Above, left*) The old Reichstag building under the wrapping designed by Christo Javacheff and his wife Jeanne-Claude, 25 June 1995. Christo began plans for the project in 1972. Half a million visitors came to see the 'wrapping' in a single weekend. (*Below, left*) The new dome of British architect Norman Foster rises behind the Quadriga of the Brandenburg Gate. (*Opposite*) Visitors stroll round the walkways of the new Reichstag building.

The German sculptor and painter Hansjörg Wagner is one of the most important German contemporary artists and philosophers of art. In the 1950s he studied with Professor Fritz Behn, himself a student of Rodin. In the 1980s he became an honorary member of the Florence Academy, other members of which have included Marino Marini and Henry Moore. He specialises in large-scale works. (*Above*) Wagner's painting of *Der Spanier* (*The Spaniard*), executed in 1983. (*Opposite*) A 1996 tempera, *Tuscan Still Life with Calla from Castle Crespina*.

Günther Grass (*above*) was born in Danzig (Gdansk) in 1927. He was a member of the Hitler Youth, was drafted into the army at the age of sixteen, and was wounded in battle. He made use of all these experiences in his first novel *Die Blechtrommel* (*The Tin Drum*), which brought him international recognition. Thirty-three years later he published *Unkenrufe*, a novel that explored the uneasy relationship between modern Germany and Poland.

(*Above, left*) Siegfried Lenz, another leading figure in German literature of the post-war period, whose best-known works include the novels *Deutschstunde* and *So zwärtlich war Suleyken*. He is seen here on 28 August 1999, when he was presented with the Goethe Prize. (*Above, right*) The prolific novelist, essayist and screenwriter Christa Wolf at the Frankfurt Book Fair, 14 October 1999. Her first novel, *Moskauer Novelle*, was published in 1961, and she established her reputation with *Der geteilte Himmel*, published three years later.

(*Left*) The German film director Wim Wenders, 24 November 1997. He originally studied medicine, but then became a student at the Munich Cinema and Television College from 1967 to 1970. Among his best-known films are *Paris, Texas*, *Wings of Desire* and *Buena Vista Social Club*.

(*Above*) Katja Riemann and Heino Ferch in a scene from Joseph Vilsmaier's 1997 film, *Comedian Harmonists*. The film is based on the lives and careers of an *acapella* band in the 1920s and 1930s. Half the members of the band were Jewish. For a while after the coming to power of the Nazis, the band continued to perform, but the day came when (like so many others) they had to seek asylum abroad.

(*Above*) Michael Schumacher speeds his Ferrari round the French Grand Prix Circuit at Nevers, 27 June 1999. It was a year in which his rivals rarely saw more than the tail fin and rear wheels of his car. (*Left*) Michael Schumacher and his Ferrari team-mate Eddie Irvine celebrate their respective 1st and 2nd places in the Monaco Grand Prix, 16 May 1999.

(*Above*) Ralf Schumacher at the wheel of his Williams-BMW car during the Spanish Grand Prix on the Circuit de Catalunya, Barcelona, 7 May 2000. (*Right*) Same day, same circuit, different team. Heinz-Harald Frentzen of the Jordan Mugen-Honda team, prepares for the Spanish Grand Prix, May 2000.

The reunited Germany presented the rest of the world with an increasingly strong challenge in almost all sports in the 1990s. No longer a split pool of talent, German sportsmen and women often proved themselves the best in the world. (*Above*) The German cyclist Jan Ullrich and members of the Team Telekom during the twenty-first and final stage of the Tour de France – somewhere between Disneyland Paris and Paris itself, 26 July 1997. (*Opposite*) The German international swimming star Franziska van Almsick lifts her body clear of the water for a swimsuit fashion photo-session, November 1992. At the Barcelona Olympics, three months earlier, van Almsick won the silver medal in the 200 metres freestyle, and the bronze medal in the 100 metres freestyle.

(*Above*) Katja Seizinger leaps down the mountain on her way to winning the gold medal in the women's downhill at the Winter Olympics in Nagano, Japan, 16 February 1998. (*Opposite*) Oliver Bierhoff (left) and Jürgen Klinsmann celebrate Germany's 2-1 World Cup victory over Mexico, Montpellier, 29 June 1998.

Index